"'*Do all the good you can; in all the ways yo*[...] John Wesley's poem describes the essence [...] caring approach will enable others to provide friendship, inclusion, and spiritual ministry for people living with dementia and their caregivers across all stages of their journey. With understanding borne from years of experience, Berry offers readers practical pathways and resources to successfully guide them on their journey of doing all the good they can to all the people they can."

—Jackie Pinkowitz, Board Chair, Dementia Action Alliance

"*When Words Fail* reflects the loving way residents with memory challenges are cared for at Westminster Canterbury, Richmond. Through the leadership of Kathy Fogg Berry and our Pastoral Care staff, our residents, their families, and our employee caregivers, are grounded in the sure knowledge that each of us is loved and remembered by God throughout every moment of our lives. It is my hope that others will be reassured of this truth and learn from this resource new ways to offer care to those with dementia and to support their families and caregivers."

—John D. Burns, President and CEO, Westminster Canterbury Richmond

As a primary caregiver for someone with dementia, and facilitator of a support group for caregivers, I have found Kathy Fogg Berry's book, *When Words Fail,* a valuable help. Her clear, user-friendly language resonates with caregivers who need such a help in their thirty-six-hour day. Her division into the three stages of dementia and helpful case studies offer the kind of help caregivers need. An added help are worship services and devotions applicable to any situation. Berry's conclusions are guides for visitors: 'Enter into the reality of the person you are visiting, help them access their faith, and never be afraid to visit someone.' If I could suggest one book for caregivers, it would be this one."

—Richard L. Morgan, caregiver, and coauthor of *No Act of Love Is Ever Wasted*

"One of the biggest challenges to improving the lives of people with dementia is helping family, friends, and community members feel comfortable interacting with the person with dementia. We are a language-dependent society. Kathy Fogg Berry understands this and opens the doors to understanding why language is difficult for someone with dementia. She teaches us how to change *our* behaviors, and how to connect with the individual based upon their retained communication skills: living in the present, listening, touch, offering experiences that appeal to the senses, music, and valuing people for who they are. This easy-to-read handbook has become a staple in my dementia-care library."

—Megan Bakan, Education and Volunteer Manager, Alzheimer's Project, Inc.

"In my work with United Methodist Churches in the Virginia Conference, I often hear from congregations who want to strengthen their caring ministries with older adults. In those conversations, more than one person will say they want to expand their visitation ministry with members who have dementia and other challenges with memory. However, most will add that they have no idea what to say or do during those visits. Their fears keep them from maintaining the connection between the faith community, the individuals, and their care partners. *When Words Fail* offers practical advice and simple steps that can encourage every person to join in this vital area of ministry. What a tremendous resource Kathy Fogg Berry provides for the local church."

—Martha E. Stokes, Director,
Church and Community Relations, Pinnacle Living

"Dementia ministries are needed in every congregation around the world, for it touches every single church out there. Kathy Fogg Berry gives practical solutions and guidance for pastors, older adult ministers, and caregivers alike. Informational and inspirational."

Hess B. "Doc" Hall, Jr.,
Director of Older Adult Spiritual Formation Programs of The Upper Room

"Vibrant and honest, *When Words Fail* addresses major concerns of people with dementia and their loved ones, focusing especially on the spiritual. Kathy Fogg Berry's years of experience as a chaplain to elders serve to provide effective approaches and words to say, recognizing that these change across the stages of dementia. Words may fail people with dementia, but those around them can learn to use effective words! Addressing churches directly, Berry provides a road map for developing a dementia ministry, using many resources they already have. I especially enjoyed the section on the use of music for coping with dementia, considering rhythm, movement, and breathing. Kathy Fogg Berry is a mentor to us all in this effort to help those with dementia maintain a connection to God, and to help the church minister through the end of life. Berry emphasizes the power of listening, and that is exactly what we should do in reading this book."

—Janice Hicks,
coauthor of *Redeeming Dementia: Spirituality, Theology, and Science*

"Faith communities are on the front lines of the dementia crisis in this country. So often, those living with dementia and their families turn first to faith leaders for solace and support. Kathy Fogg Berry is a leading voice on the vital importance of continued spiritual life of those with dementia. Based on her decades of experience and success in improving quality of life and continuing spiritual engagement, Berry offers practical advice for communities of all faiths to ensure that those impacted by dementia and their care partners can continue faith practices as valued members of their communities."

—Virginia Biggar, Executive Director, Faith United Against Alzheimer's Coalition

"All of us are only a few degrees of separation from someone living with dementia among our family, friends, and spiritual circles. Kathy Fogg Berry's pastoral experience and theological knowledge as a chaplain in a senior living community gives her a rich and valuable perspective to address this crucial issue. In her book, *When Words Fail*, she explains dementia in understandable ways and encourages readers like us to take action with compassion and hope. Read this book, keep it close, and refer to it often. You'll find an invaluable resource that will help you lean in and support those with dementia and their care partners."

—Cynthia Ray, Executive Director,
PAHSA: Presbyterian Association of Homes & Services for the Aging

WHEN
Words
FAIL

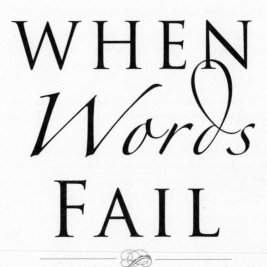

Practical Ministry to People with
Dementia and Their Caregivers

KATHY FOGG BERRY

Kregel
Ministry

When Words Fail: Practical Ministry to People with Dementia and Their Caregivers

Published by Kregel Ministry, an imprint of Kregel Publications, 2450 Oak Industrial Dr. NE, Grand Rapids, MI 49505.

Published in association with the literary agency of WordServe Literary Group, Ltd., www.wordserveliterary.com.

Photographs by Eric A. Futterman. Used with permission.

The image on page 25 is taken from Blausen.com staff. Blausen gallery 2014. Wikiversity Journal of Medicine. DOI:10.15347/wjm/2014.010. ISSN 20018762 (Own work) [CC BY 3.0 (http://creativecommons.org/licenses/by/3.0)], via Wikimedia Commons.

The authors and publisher are not engaged in rendering medical or psychological services, and this book is not intended as a guide to diagnose or treat medical or psychological problems. If medical, psychological, or other expert assistance is required, the reader should seek the services of a health-care provider or certified counselor.

The persons and events portrayed in this book have been used with permission. To protect the privacy of these individuals, in many cases, names and identifying details have been changed, and multiple stories have been combined to create one vignette.

ISBN 978-0-8254-4559-0

Printed in the United States of America

18 19 20 21 22 / 5 4 3 2 1

Dedicated to those who live on in the memory of God, who never forgets.

CONTENTS

ACKNOWLEDGMENTS

⸺ ☙ ⸺

For nearly a decade, I have worked with residents living with dementia at Westminster Canterbury Richmond, a continuing care retirement community in Richmond, Virginia, originally founded through an alliance of regional Presbyterian and Episcopal entities. Thanks to the vision of Rev. W. Ray Inscoe, now Chaplain Emeritus of Westminster Canterbury Richmond, and the support of generous donors through Westminster Canterbury Foundation, I began work in 2009 as the chaplain dedicated to memory care. Having worked as a chaplain in several long-term care settings, and as a trainer for the Alzheimer's Association, I knew more could be done to develop spiritual ministry to those with dementia. The opportunity to cultivate that idea grew and blossomed at Westminster Canterbury Richmond.

Westminster Canterbury Richmond dedicates itself to excellence and compassion in equal measure, and has recognized that memory care is a critical area of service to be explored and developed. It is a place that takes its roots in faith seriously, and is a vibrant place that strives to integrate a rich variety of programs to ensure the best life possible for every resident. A child development center enables intergenerational magic between residents and children. The campus theater features performers from around the globe, and residents enjoy numerous studio art opportunities. Residents are supported by a wide variety of pastoral care offerings every week. All of this is available to every resident, including those in memory care.

Dementia diseases are on the rise. This reality, and its implications, spurred the organization toward finding ways to help current and future residents, caregivers, and church families deal with the impending wave. Westminster Canterbury Richmond has three distinct levels of memory care living. Throughout these areas of residence, they employ caring nursing and recreational staff who are experts in their field. Each week, memory care residents benefit from multiple offerings of music, art, horticulture, and exercise therapies designed to significantly improve quality of life.

But more significantly for you, our reader, Westminster Canterbury is an incubator for effective interactions and a testing ground for supportive approaches for families, churches, and residents alike. Through collaborative work, we have been able to engage families, clergy, volunteers, interns, and staff in discovering how to help residents cope with the real and devastating effects of dementia. It was into this unusually fertile soil that the *When Words Fail* book, DVD, and study guide were realized. (The DVD and downloadable study guide are available separately at www.whenwordsfail.com.)

This project was made possible by an innovation grant from LeadingAge, a national affiliation of senior living providers, and a generous anonymous donor whose spouse suffered a long journey through Alzheimer's disease. In deciding to support this project our donor spoke this truth: "Dementia *is* a spiritual issue. Regardless of your faith affiliation, it starts with a fear so deep it rocks you. And that is a spiritual experience in need of help!"

Along with thanking LeadingAge and the visionary donor for supporting *When Words Fail*, I want to thank others who have provided invaluable input. Gayle Hunter Haglund, Director Resource Development for Westminster Canterbury Richmond, tirelessly sought and attained the financial support needed for this project to become reality. Gayle, who contributed content, research, and editing, recognized the need for a chapter on the church-wide response to dementia care and composed much of its content. She and Lynn McClintock, Director of Pastoral Care for Westminster Canterbury Richmond, provided excellent editorial critique of the book, guidance, and support throughout the project.

Much gratitude goes to Keely Latcham Boeving, a gifted editor, and to Eric Futterman, President of EAF Communication, for the beautiful photography. Eric produced the book's companion DVD, which provides valuable information about spiritual care and dementia, and demonstrates pastoral care visits with people experiencing dementia (again, available at www.whenwordsfail.com, along with downloadable study guide). Although the video and guide were designed for use in groups, it would also be beneficial for individuals seeking to serve those with dementia.

I am grateful to past and present pastoral care teammates at Westminster Canterbury, who are a blessing to minister alongside and a constant source of encouragement. Daily I learn from excellent memory support staff who allow me to serve with them to enhance resident well-being, and together provide precious person-centered care to residents.

Along with those at Westminster Canterbury Richmond, I thank the colleagues, residents, patients and families with whom I have been privileged to work and learn from at Virginia Commonwealth University Health System, the Masonic Home of Virginia, The Virginia Home, and Bon Secours Hospice. The Greater Richmond Chapter of the Alzheimer's Association staff in Richmond, Virginia, initially trained me in dementia care and then allowed me to train others with them. I cannot thank them enough for all they have taught me and all they do daily to support people living with dementia and their caregivers.

Early in my Clinical Pastoral Education (CPE) training at VCU Health Systems, Marlyne Cain, my supervisor and mentor, recognized and nurtured my love for older adults which has grown into a passionate ministry. She connected me with Dr. Sultan Lakhani, who welcomed me onto his geriatric psychiatry team as a student chaplain. I learned so much from that team about dementia and its effects on individuals and their families.

I'm very appreciative of readers Daniel Felty, MD; Debbie Perkins, NP; and Laura Mohun, RN; who made sure medical information was accurate. Friends Laurie Graham and Malinda Collier graciously read the manuscript and offered not only valuable insights, but nerve-calming encouragement. Candace McKibben has encouraged my writing and supported my dreams through decades of friendship.

My family deserve more thanks than I can ever express—Bill, Micah, Amber, Mary-Catherine, Elizabeth, and Whitt—for listening to me talk about this idea for years and encouraging me. Most importantly, though, I'm thankful to God for the gift of this ministry and to residents and families who allow me to walk alongside them, offering spiritual support.

INTRODUCTION

*D*andelion puffs have always fascinated me. Bright yellow petals eventually give way to fluffy, seed-bearing flower heads that are randomly scattered by gentle breaths or breezes. Watching seed tufts drift on the wind is magical. Sometimes the flower head swiftly empties as seeds disperse, while other times a few seeds frantically cling on until the next wave of wind.

While ministering to people living with dementia for the last seventeen years as a chaplain and trainer for the Alzheimer's Association, I have often been reminded of dandelions. Like dandelion seed puffs drifting on the wind, gradually memories drift away, lost on the currents of relentless dementia diseases. The random nature of brain cell death, which causes dementia, is unique to each person. The timing of brain changes leading to lost memories and abilities is also unique to each person. While many memories drift away, some cling stubbornly on, mysteriously enabling a person to catch glimpses of the past or recall fragments of reality.

Although memories are gradually lost for people living with dementia, people are never lost to the memory of God. Nor should they be lost to their faith communities. Sadly, though, as memories fade and conversation becomes more difficult due to word-finding and speaking difficulty, visitors from faith communities sometimes stop visiting their parishioners who have a dementia disease. This is not due to lack of caring, but when words begin to fail for people with dementia, they sometimes fail for visitors who don't know what to say or what to do.

This book can help. It is a practical book, rooted in my own experience of years of trial and error while ministering to people in various stages of dementia diseases. In these pages you'll find information and tools designed to help you move from a sense of helplessness to a place where you feel equipped to address and care for the spiritual needs of those living with dementia diseases.

WHY IS THIS RESOURCE NEEDED?

We are all wonderful creations of God and need to be valued and loved. Sadly, society seems to value people because of what they can do and not for who they are. As people lose their cognition and functional abilities due to dementia diseases, they too often begin to feel devalued by others and to devalue themselves. This leaves them hurting and in need of love and support. There are more than 5 million Americans living with Alzheimer's disease today[1]—to say nothing of the many other types of dementia diseases—and many of these men and women are vital parts of our congregations and church communities. They need to be reminded of their importance to God and to us. They need to be reminded of God's presence and unconditional love.

This book is written from the vantage point of pastoral and spiritual care. Though general medical information about causes of dementia and stages of disease are provided, this is not intended, nor should the reader rely upon this, as medical advice. Following a chapter about the physiology of dementia, you'll find chapters breaking dementia diseases into three general stages. It is important to note that these stages are generalities. Not every person living with dementia progresses through these stages, and if they do, they don't progress with the same timing or with the same effects. There are enough commonalities, though, to make observations and recommendations that will benefit people experiencing dementia, their caregivers and the people seeking to serve them.

This book contains vital information from the national Alzheimer's Association and its resources. This organization tirelessly champions research, provides education and offers invaluable support to people living with Alzheimer's and other dementia diseases, as well as to their caregivers.

While *When Words Fail* emphasizes how dementia affects people physically, emotionally, and spiritually, the book's focus is on providing practical tools to help you minister to people with dementia. These are practices I've tried and found to be very effective for providing holistic care—ministering to the mind, body, and soul. You'll also receive practical suggestions on how to communicate, eventually without words. Taken together, these tools will give you a better understanding of how to visit and support not only the people living with dementia but their caregivers, too. I pray that faith communities will awaken to rich ministry opportunities so desperately needed for people with dementia, and for families coping with these challenges.

You wouldn't be checking out this resource if Christ's call in Matthew 25, to minister to "the least of these," wasn't touching your heart. May you find what you need in these humble pages.

Chapter 1

WHEN WORDS FAIL:
WHAT DO WE DO?

Mr. Clarke has Alzheimer's disease and never sits still. He spends his days pacing the halls. But when traditional hymns are played, he sits and quietly listens, as if he's been transported to church.

Mrs. Brown, who has vascular dementia, is always anxious. The only time her anxiety lessens and sometimes stops is when someone prays with her. Then, her face transforms into an image of peace and contentment.

Mrs. Wells has Alzheimer's disease and can no longer converse. But when the Lord's Prayer or the 23rd Psalm is led, she recites it from beginning to end.

*S*tatistics reveal that about 72 percent of people over seventy-five years of age consider their faith to be very important to them.[1] Yet one-third of people over eighty-five have Alzheimer's disease,[2] and nearly half have some form of dementia, making them increasingly unable to participate in religious organizations or initiate faith practices that comfort, reconnect and uplift them. They need clergy, lay church leaders, fellow church members, and professional and family caregivers to help them practice their faith. Over time, those with dementia diseases become dependent on others to initiate important faith practices and to nurture relationships. This is where we, as members of a faith community, come in.

It may initially feel awkward to communicate with someone as they progress further into dementia, becoming increasingly unable to communicate with words. When the person living with dementia loses vocal communication ability, too often those who visit them struggle to connect. As dementia progresses, visitors often stop coming, feeling their time won't make a difference. The person with advanced dementia may not recognize even a frequent visitor or remember they were there. We begin to wonder: Does it matter if I visit?

It matters a lot!

Without us, vital connections are lost. Whether or not people remember a visit is not important. What is important is the visit itself, which provides love and connection. What is important is living in the moment with people who have a dementia disease. In that moment you show your love for them and remind them of God's love and presence. What is important is creating a sacred space and helping them tap into their faith. What is important, even if they will have forgotten the visit five minutes later, are those moments of connection they have with you—and with God *through* you. What matters is their relationship with God and with you.

When Words Fail will help equip you to make those connections—to reach out to those living with dementia and offer person-centered spiritual care.

You may have noticed some people in your church beginning to have memory issues.

Perhaps a Sunday school teacher, who has taught for thirty years, is beginning to repeat lessons and class members are complaining.

Maybe an elderly deacon frequently looks confused and forgets what to do when taking up the offering.

An older woman in your church may repeatedly show up for Sunday worship service on Thursday morning. When you explain that it's Thursday, she gets upset and leaves in a huff.

Perhaps your seasoned church treasurer has been making incorrect entries of offerings, confusing the ledger, and refusing to see his mistakes when pointed out.

You may have noticed an active church leader gradually disappearing to take care of her husband, who's "not well." You've seen how he doesn't interact with folks at church anymore, but you don't really know what's wrong because she won't talk about it.

These exact scenarios may not be occurring at your church, but no doubt dementia is touching your congregants in some way, whether through family, friends, coworkers, or neighbors. It's inescapable. In some cases, the presence of dementia in your congregation may not even be noticeable yet—but in all likelihood, it's there. People living with dementia diseases, as well as other mental health diseases, often feel stigmatized by society and hide their struggles for fear of misunderstanding and rejection. This is a travesty. At a time when they desperately need to feel God's loving embrace through us, they often don't.

Alzheimer's disease and other dementias are not acute illnesses. They are long-term, and often progressively debilitating. The average length of time someone lives with Alzheimer's disease is eight years, but it could be as much as twenty years or more. The longevity of these diseases provides a challenge for churches. Churches are more used to addressing acute needs, things such as pneumonia, cancer, a broken leg, heart attack, or the flu virus. These are illnesses and problems that, when addressed, are fixable within a few days, weeks, or months. Ministering to people with dementia diseases is a long-term commitment that takes intentionality and persistence.

Churches should not expect their ministers to do all visitation. Caring for the congregation is the whole church's responsibility. This is especially needed since dementia diseases have such longevity, and the tenure of a church's minister may not be as long as the illness. It will take time for a new minister to build a relationship with someone in advanced stages of dementia and her caregiver. Congregation members who have been faithfully visiting can help smooth this transition and provide consistent care.

Ministry to people with dementia needs to involve church members with knowledge and ability to minister long-term. Forming a team of pastoral caregivers can help meet this need. It takes a village. Committed people are needed to walk alongside those living with dementia diseases and their caregivers for the long haul.

A TEAM APPROACH

Your church may already have a team of congregational caregivers such as a pastoral care team, Befrienders, Stephen Ministers, or deacons. If so, some of those team members may feel called to minister to people living with dementia and their caregivers. If your church doesn't have such teams in place, consider forming a team specifically designed for this type of ministry. Enlist interested people through the newsletter, Sunday school class, pulpit announcements or other communication mediums in your church. Once a group convenes, offer educational opportunities for team members to learn about dementia and how to care for people living with dementia diseases. Use this book and its accompanying DVD, resources located in the back of the book, speakers from your local Alzheimer's chapter, and the wisdom of caregivers from your church and community who have cared for people experiencing dementia.

Once your team has a general understanding of what it means to care for those with dementia diseases, spend time discovering team members' gifts and skills for ministry. Some people may be interested in visiting and offering emotional and spiritual support, while others may want to provide such things as meals, rides to appointments, running errands, or conducting home repair. Encourage the team to spend time in prayer, asking for God's guidance and leadership as this valuable ministry unfolds. Enlist team members to discern people in need of support within your congregation and community.

As you take steps to create this ministry, ask the team to consider what the church's role is when people inside your church, and in your community, begin experiencing debilitating memory loss but have no caregivers to care for them. They may have no siblings, spouses, children, nieces, nephews, or friends with the ability to address their needs. Does the church share responsibility to help in situations like this? If so, what do we do?

In John 21:17, Peter asked Christ what the Lord wanted him to do. Christ replied, "Feed My sheep." *Take care of my people.* Throughout the New Testament we find this biblical mandate expressed in many different ways. This is our call. May we be faithful.

Chapter 2

DEMENTIA: WHAT IS IT?

Dementia.

*I*t is a term we hear often, used as a label for a wide variety of symptoms that express themselves in many different ways. Unfortunately, the broad brush stroke of the word often leaves us with little clarity. What does it actually mean?

Think of dementia as the umbrella under which eighty to ninety different types of memory-related diseases reside. Dementia is a general term for loss of memory and other mental abilities severe enough to interfere with daily life. It is caused by physical changes in the brain, which affect each person uniquely. Specifically, it is a result of damage to brain cells (neurons). This damage interferes with the ability of brain cells to communicate with each other—and when they cannot communicate normally, thinking, behaviors, feelings, and actions are affected.

At this time a cure for dementia diseases does not exist, but individuals, institutions, research associations, and the government are pouring millions of dollars into finding one. In the meantime, there are medications available that can reduce the severity of symptoms and behaviors but, unfortunately, they only work with certain types of dementia and for a limited period of time.

Although having dementia is *not* a normal part of aging, one in five people aged sixty-five and older worldwide, in developed countries, has some form of dementia. While symptoms of dementia vary greatly, at least two of the following core mental functions must be significantly impaired for a person to be considered to have dementia: memory, communication and language, ability to focus and pay attention, reasoning and judgment, and visual perception.[1]

WHAT'S HAPPENING IN THE BRAIN?

The brain is composed of three parts: the cerebrum, cerebellum, and brain stem. These different parts of the brain control aspects of a person's personality and abilities to function. When cells in a particular region are damaged, that region cannot carry out its functions normally or interact normally with other regions of the brain. As has been said before, dementia affects everyone differently, as different parts of the brain are affected at different times in each person. Nevertheless, understanding how the brain works and how it is oftentimes progressively affected by the disease can help make sense of how people living with dementia diseases communicate, react, and respond.

The **cerebrum** is divided into four distinct lobes responsible for different functions, such as memory, judgment, communication, movement, and sight.

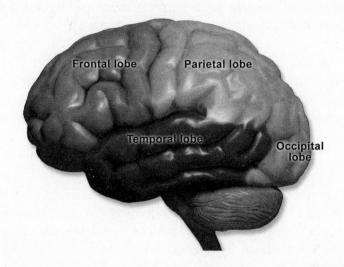

The **frontal lobe** is the control center. An individual's personality, intelligence, and ability to emote reside here, as does short-term memory. This lobe enables a person to, among other things, plan, reason, make appropriate choices and decisions, problem-solve, speak and write, understand what should and should not be done, discern what is appropriate and what is not, concentrate, move, and think. When dementia affects this part of the brain, a person might repeat stories, fail to perform tasks that were once part of their normal routine, or act irrationally or impulsively out of character to his or her normal self.

The **temporal lobe** is the language center. It has two sides, one on each side of the brain. Each side affects different aspects of a person's ability to communicate. This part of the brain enables a person to do such things as understand language; find words; hear, sequence, and understand what others are saying; and respond appropriately. Most people living with dementia diseases have brain cell damage in both sides of the temporal lobe, thus explaining why so many experience language difficulties.

The **parietal lobe** controls such things as sense of touch; perception of stimuli; ability to distinguish size, shape, and color; and orientation. Brain cell damage due to dementia in this part of the brain explains why some people experience things like thinking objects are closer or further away than they really are or being overly sensitive to touch.

The **occipital lobe** is the visual processing center. It controls a person's ability to see and to process what is seen. Sometimes people lose their peripheral vision and suffer from tunnel vision as dementia diseases progress. They may think objects or shadows are real people or animals.

IS IT ALWAYS DEMENTIA?

Tom, an eighty-eight-year-old retired navy pilot, hasn't been himself lately. Usually even-tempered and mild-mannered, he's suddenly become argumentative and even delusional at times. He can't sit still and is confused. His wife, Meg, is very concerned. Their daughters think he's getting dementia and want him tested. First, Tom's doctor orders a urine analysis and blood work. It turns out Tom has a urinary tract infection (UTI). Once infection-fighting medication gets into his system, he soon returns to being himself.

Ruby usually loves interacting with her grandchildren and great-grandchildren, but now she seems sullen and withdrawn. Tasks that used to be simple for her, like baking cookies, are impossible. Ruby stares at ingredients and doesn't know what to do with them. When she talks, her words are halting, and she sometimes has trouble saying the correct word for something she wants. Her son takes her to the doctor, fearing the onset of Alzheimer's disease. After blood work, a CT scan and other medical tests, it is discovered that Ruby has a brain tumor. The tumor is causing the personality and ability shifts Ruby is experiencing.

Like Tom and Ruby, in some cases individuals do not have a dementia disease but instead a physiological condition with symptoms that mimic those of a dementia disease. Some common causes of dementia-like symptoms are depression, delirium, infections, side effects from medication, thyroid problems, certain vitamin deficiencies, urinary tract infections, tumors, drug interactions, and excessive use of alcohol. Unlike dementia diseases, these conditions may be reversed with treatment. Before definitively diagnosing a dementia disease, doctors first rule out potentially reversible physiological causes for cognitive problems.

DEMENTIA'S MANY FORMS

The brain can malfunction in various ways—and as we saw above, malfunctions are not necessarily an indication of brain cell death or of the onset of a dementia disease. If other causes can be ruled out, however, it is likely that a person may be suffering from one of the various nonreversible types of dementia diseases affecting millions of people worldwide today. There are many manifestations of these diseases, each of which affect people in different ways. Sadly, all of these incurable diseases are robbing people of treasured memories and important relational abilities.

Alzheimer's Disease

According to the Alzheimer's Association, Alzheimer's disease is the most common cause of dementia, affecting 60 to 80 percent of people with dementia diseases.[2] A degenerative brain disease, it occurs when nerve cells (neurons) in the brain involved in cognitive function have been damaged and no longer function normally. This damage eventually affects parts of the brain that enable a person to carry out basic bodily functions such as communicating, walking and, eventually, swallowing. People in the final stages of the disease are often bed-bound and require total care. With Alzheimer's disease, as well as other dementia diseases, people die from medical complications in addition to their dementia disease such as heart attack, stroke, pneumonia or other serious complications.

A Serious National Problem[3]

- In the United States, Alzheimer's is the sixth leading cause of death.
- In 2016 an estimated 5.4 million Americans have Alzheimer's disease.
- One in nine people age sixty-five and older (11 percent) has Alzheimer's disease. Alarmingly, every sixty-six seconds someone in the United States develops Alzheimer's disease.

- By 2025, the number of people age sixty-five and older with Alzheimer's disease is estimated to reach 7.1 million, a nearly 40 percent increase from 2016. Barring the development of medical breakthroughs to prevent or cure the disease, the number will rise to 13.6 million by 2050.
- Payments for health care for individuals are estimated at $226 billion.

OTHER DEMENTIA DISEASES

While Alzheimer's disease is the most common and widely recognized dementia disease, it is not the only one. It is important to recognize that the many different dementia diseases present varying symptoms and require varying types of treatment. You may have congregants or others in your community who display symptoms similar to Alzheimer's disease but ultimately have one of the eighty to ninety other forms of dementia. Below you will find a few of the more prevalent dementia diseases, as detailed in Alzheimer's Association resources.[4]

Mild Cognitive Impairment (MCI)

In MCI, a person has problems with memory or one of the other core functions affected by dementia, such as language, focus, or visual perception. These problems are severe enough to be noticeable to other people and to show up on tests of mental function, but not serious enough to interfere with daily life. When symptoms do not disrupt daily activities, a person does not meet criteria for being diagnosed with dementia. The best-studied type of MCI involves difficulty with memory.

Individuals with MCI have an increased risk of developing Alzheimer's disease after a few years, especially when their main problem involves memory. However, not everyone diagnosed with MCI progresses to Alzheimer's or another kind of dementia.

Vascular Dementia

Many experts consider vascular dementia the second-most-common type of dementia disease, after Alzheimer's disease. It occurs when clots block blood flow to parts of the brain, depriving nerve cells of food and oxygen. If it develops soon after a single major stroke blocks a large blood vessel, it is sometimes called "post-stroke dementia."

Vascular dementia can also occur when a series of very small strokes, or infarcts, clog tiny blood vessels. Individually, these strokes do not cause major symptoms, but over time their combined effect is damaging. This type of vascular dementia used to be called "multi-infarct dementia."

Symptoms of vascular dementia can vary, depending on the brain regions involved. Forgetfulness may or may not be a promi-nent symptom, depending on whether memory areas are affected. Other common symptoms include confusion and difficulty focusing attention. Decline in a person with vascular dementia may occur in "steps," where there is a fairly sudden change in function.

People who develop vascular dementia may have a history of heart attacks. High blood pressure or cholesterol, diabetes, or other risk factors for heart disease are often present.

Mixed Dementia

In mixed dementia, Alzheimer's disease and vascular demen-tia occur at the same time. Many experts believe mixed dementia develops more often than was previously realized and that it may become increasingly common as people age. This belief is based on autopsies showing that the brains of up to 45 percent of people with dementia have signs of both Alzheimer's and vascular disease.

Decline in people with mixed dementia may follow a pattern similar to either Alzheimer's or vascular dementia, or a combination of the two. Experts suggest that the possibility for mixed dementia is high whenever a person has both evidence of cardiovascular disease and dementia symptoms that worsen slowly.

Dementia with Lewy Bodies (DLB)

In DLB, abnormal deposits of a protein called alpha-synuclein form inside the brain's nerve cells. These deposits are called "Lewy bodies" after the scientist who first described them. Lewy bodies have been found in several brain disorders, including dementia with Lewy bodies, Parkinson's disease, and some cases of Alzheimer's.

Symptoms of DLB include memory problems, poor judgment, confusion, and other symptoms that can overlap with Alzheimer's disease. Movement symptoms are also common, including stiffness, shuffling walk, shakiness, lack of facial expression, and problems with balance and falls. People with this illness may also experience excessive daytime drowsiness and visual hallucinations. Mental symptoms and level of alertness may fluctuate during the day or from one day to another.

In about 50 percent of cases, DLB is associated with a condition called rapid eye movement (REM) sleep disorder. REM sleep is the stage of sleep in which people usually dream. During normal REM sleep, body movement is blocked and people do not "act out" their dreams. In REM sleep disorder, movements are not blocked and people act out their dreams, sometimes vividly and violently.

Parkinson's Disease

Parkinson's is another disease involving Lewy bodies. The cells that are damaged and destroyed in Parkinson's are chiefly in a brain area important in controlling movement. Symptoms include tremors and shakiness; stiffness; difficulty with walking, muscle control, and balance; lack of facial expression; and impaired speech. Many individuals with Parkinson's develop dementia in later stages of the disease.

Frontotemporal Dementia (FTD)

FTD is a rare disorder chiefly affecting the front and sides of the brain. Because these regions often (but not always) shrink, brain imaging can help in diagnosis. Usually there is no specific abnormality found in the brain in FTD; however, in one type, called Pick's disease, there are sometimes abnormal microscopic deposits called Pick bodies.

FTD progresses more quickly than Alzheimer's disease and tends to occur at a younger age. The first symptoms often involve changes in personality, judgment, planning, and social skills. Individuals may make rude or off-color remarks to family or strangers, or make unwise decisions about finances or personal matters. They may show feelings disconnected from the situation, such as indifference or excessive excitement. They may have an unusually strong urge to eat and thus gain weight as a result.

Creutzfeldt-Jakob Disease (CJD)

Creutzfeldt-Jakob disease (pronounced CROYZ-felt YAH-cob) is a rare, rapidly fatal disorder affecting about one in a million people per year worldwide. It usually affects individuals older than sixty. CJD is one of the prion (PREE-awn) diseases—disorders that occur when prion protein, a protein normally present in the brain, begins to fold into an abnormal three-dimensional shape. This shape gradually triggers the protein throughout the brain to fold into the same abnormal shape, leading to increasing damage and destruction of brain cells.

Recently, scientists identified "variant Creutzfeldt-Jakob disease" (vCJD) as the human disorder believed to be caused by eating meat from cattle affected by "mad cow disease." It tends to occur in much younger individuals, in some cases as early as their teens.

The first symptoms of CJD may involve impairment in memory, thinking, and reasoning, or changes in personality and behavior. Depression or agitation also tend to occur early. Problems with movement may be present from the beginning or appear shortly after the other symptoms. CJD progresses rapidly and is usually fatal within a year.

Normal Pressure Hydrocephalus (NPH)

Normal pressure hydrocephalus is another rare disorder in which fluid surrounding the brain and spinal cord is unable to drain normally. The fluid builds up, enlarging the ventricles (fluid-filled chambers) inside the brain. As the chambers expand, they compress and damage nearby tissue. "Normal pressure" refers to the fact that the spinal fluid pressure often still falls within the normal range on a spinal tap.

The three chief symptoms of NPH are difficulty walking, loss of bladder control, and mental decline, usually involving an overall slowing in understanding and reacting to information. A person's responses are delayed, but they tend to be accurate and appropriate to the situation when they finally come.

NPH can occasionally be treated by surgically inserting a long, thin tube called a shunt to drain fluid from the brain to the abdomen.

Certain television broadcasts and commercials have portrayed NPH as a highly treatable condition that is often misdiagnosed as Alzheimer's or Parkinson's disease. However, most experts believe it is unlikely that significant numbers of people diagnosed with Alzheimer's or Parkinson's actually have a form of NPH that could be corrected with surgery. NPH is rare, and it looks different from Alzheimer's or Parkinson's to a physician with experience in assessing brain disorders. When shunting surgery is successful, it tends to help more with walking and bladder control than with mental decline.

Huntington's Disease

Huntington's disease is a fatal brain disorder caused by inherited changes in a single gene. These changes lead to destruction of nerve cells in certain brain regions. Anyone with a parent with Huntington's has a 50 percent chance of inheriting the gene, and everyone who inherits it will eventually develop the disorder. In about 1 to 3 percent of cases, no history of the disease can be found in other family members. The age when symptoms develop and the rate of progression vary.

Symptoms of Huntington's disease include twitches, spasms, and other involuntary movements; problems with balance and coordination; personality changes; and trouble with memory, concentration, or making decisions.

While the conditions laid out above are some of the more common manifestations of dementia diseases, they barely scratch the surface of the many forms the disease can take. Despite the differences in symptoms, it is not always easy to identify which type of dementia a person has. Careful observation and testing must occur and sometimes it is still difficult to delineate what exactly is happening in the complex brain of an individual. This can be a challenging time for those who have begun to notice symptoms, often relating to their short-term memory, and have sought out a physician to help discover what's going on. The following chapter talks about the often challenging road to receiving a dementia disease diagnosis.

Chapter 3

OBTAINING A DIAGNOSIS

Phil Hall is just not himself. His wife, Martha, knows it. At seventy years old, Phil retired from his construction business and Martha retired from her nursing job. For the last couple of years they enjoyed traveling in their RV, visiting state parks and friends along the way. They recently celebrated their fiftieth wedding anniversary with a huge party and are in the prime of their life, or so they thought.

Over the last few years, Martha has noticed that Phil has been forgetting things. At first, it wasn't a big deal to find misplaced keys or reschedule a few missed appointments, but now his short-term memory is quickly failing him. He has begun accusing Martha of not telling him things that she has told him several times. He is repeating questions, forgetting the way to familiar places when driving, and paying bills twice or not at all.

As facilities committee chairperson for their church, he is also not getting things fixed in a timely way. This is not typical of Phil, ordinarily a well-organized, dependable man. People are beginning to notice and to ask Martha what's going on.

Out of concern, Martha talks to the family doctor and their children. The doctor, who usually sees Phil for ten or fifteen minutes in his office, reports that he hasn't seen a cognitive problem. The children, who live out of town, also say they don't see a problem. They come for day visits every couple of months. Phil is very social and covers his memory loss well when reminiscing or playing with the grandchildren.

When Phil learns that Martha has talked with their children and the doctor, he becomes very angry and distressed, denying any problem and accusing Martha of making things up. Martha is feeling overwhelmed and frustrated. She doesn't know who to turn to.

Charlotte Burns, at eighty, is very physically and socially active. Recently, though, she's been experiencing some memory loss and good-naturedly points it out during awkward moments with family when she makes mistakes. In conversation she often stops, mid-question, to ask if she's asked the question before. If she has, she apologizes and blames her waning memory. Out of self-concern, she's made an appointment with her doctor to discuss the memory loss

she's experiencing. She believes in facing things head-on and getting the help she needs.

Charlotte's family is grateful for her positive attitude and willingness to face whatever might be going on. They are happy to help any way needed, but know how independent she is about taking care of herself.

*E*ach of these scenarios is realistic. Understandably, people react to memory loss as individually as to anything else in life. Some people, like Phil, deny problems or cannot see them in themselves. Some people, like Charlotte, acknowledge problems and seek solutions.

When people begin to notice memory loss in themselves, for most it is a very scary and disorienting time. Because of the societal stigma attached to any sort of mental health problem, people work hard to hide memory deficits or confusion. When keeping up with conversations and social graces becomes too taxing, some begin staying home from social engagements or church. They begin to feel isolated and alone, even in a group, because fully participating becomes too difficult. Unintentionally, others don't often notice their difficulty and fail to reach out, which leaves people dealing with memory loss feeling further removed.

When ministering to people in the early stages of memory loss and their families, listening is the key. We must listen not just with our ears, but with our eyes and hearts as well. Ministers and people caring for others need to create a safe and confidential space where people experiencing memory loss, and their caregivers, can talk and even rant. They need the freedom to feel and express whatever emotions they are experiencing—to question God, if needed—and to know they have a trusted confidant to turn to. They need us to listen nonjudgmentally and confidentially. Building a trusting relationship as they begin this journey will increase the likelihood that we will be allowed to walk with them throughout its progression.

While getting an accurate dementia diagnosis can help some come to terms with their symptoms, this process can take years. At first, memory loss may be slight and not significantly interfere with life, enabling the sufferer to largely ignore it. For some, the journey begins with a diagnosis of mild cognitive impairment. Memory is compromised, but not one's ability to perform essential activities of daily living (ADLs). Many people progress from a mild cognitive impairment diagnosis into a dementia disease.

No single, simple test exists to diagnose a dementia disease. Instead, acquiring a diagnosis is an involved and timely process requiring doctors to use a variety of approaches and methods. Often, getting a diagnosis involves a process of elimination to rule out what is not going on before an affirmative dementia disease diagnosis is made. To obtain a definitive diagnosis, a primary care doctor will often acquire a medical and family history from the individual, including psychiatric history and a history of cognitive and behavioral changes.[1]

The doctor will often ask family members or other people close to the individual to provide input about changes in thinking skills or behavior. It will be necessary to perform a physical examination and order lab work, and to seek input from specialists, such as a neurologist and neuropsychologist, who will conduct neurologic examinations and cognitive testing. Often the physician will order a magnetic resonance imaging (MRI) scan that can help identify brain changes, such as a tumor, that could explain the individual's symptoms.

Doctors can determine that a person has dementia with a high level of certainty. It's harder, though, to determine the exact type of dementia because symptoms and brain changes related to different dementia diseases can overlap. In many cases, a primary care doctor may diagnose "dementia" and not specify a type. A neurologist may provide more clarity.

To gather as much information as possible, doctors are dependent on input from the patient, if possible, and family caregivers. Caregivers might keep a journal of cognitive and behavioral changes they witness in their loved one. It can be helpful to share such a journal with the doctor ahead of a visit so observed changes and challenges aren't discussed in front of the loved one.

Second opinions may be needed, and sometimes patients will be given a referral to a neurologist, a specialist who specifically deals with neurologic brain changes. At a neurologist's office, cognitive testing as well as physical and neurological exams occur. Even those test results can sometimes be inconclusive in the beginning stages, however. A person can test well but still be having difficulties in daily functioning, which the test may not see. This can cause frustration for the person suffering from memory loss and their loved ones, who may feel unheard or misunderstood.

For these reasons and many others, it is essential for people experiencing cognitive decline and their caregivers to have someone to talk to. They need support as they make decisions regarding future plans and care. They need encouragement, assurance of God's presence, and care from trusted clergy and friends. In order for compassionate and understanding support to occur, it is important to recognize the emotions that surface when people receive a dementia diagnosis and progress through the different stages of dementia diseases.

Phil and Charlotte, introduced earlier in the chapter, depict people experiencing different emotions as a dementia disease enters their lives. Emotional responses to life situations are different for everyone. They are based on personalities, families of origin, coping skills, life experiences, and more. When seeking to effectively minister to people with dementia diseases and their families, we must be aware of and sensitive to emotions and feelings surrounding the struggle to get a diagnosis, and the ensuing emotions once one is received. Everyone is entitled to feel however they feel; your role is to be present with them regardless. The following emotions are common responses that you might encounter in people when receiving a dementia diagnosis and as brain changes progress.

COMMON EMOTIONS EXPERIENCED

Confusion

Before others notice something is wrong, the person experiencing memory loss can tell things just aren't right. Everyday tasks that used to be simple get mixed up: driving to the doctor he's gone to for years or to her regular hair salon is full of unfamiliar detours; biscuits she made from scratch don't rise the same thanks to missing ingredients; replacing a slipping fan belt becomes a tangled mess for someone who used to do it in minutes. Confusion multiplies as memory becomes cloudier and the person experiencing memory loss understandably tries to maintain normalcy. This is tiring and overwhelming, though, and confusion becomes like a snowball heading downhill, out of control.

Embarrassment

People in the beginning stages of a dementia disease often realize they are losing control. They're aware that they often feel confused and disoriented. As this confusion starts to impact how they relate to others and interact in social settings, they often begin to pull back from interacting, for fear they'll do or say something wrong. Unfortunately, many receive "the look" (a rolling of the eyes or judging stare) from someone when they repeat a story, ask the same questions, or come to church dressed inappropriately. They are very aware of negative or judgmental responses they receive from others. Our faith communities need to be educated about dementia, its symptoms, and its emotional and spiritual impacts on those who suffer from it. When people know how those living with dementia diseases are affected, they can respond more compassionately and with greater understanding. Embarrassment can be avoided.

Denial

In the early stages of dementia diseases, a person can appear clear-minded one day and cloudy the next. Changes in behavior and memories can occur within the hour, too. In the beginning, the person may be able to function normally most of the time, continuing to carry on social conversations and function in situations that don't require complex decision making. This may allow him to deny the presence of a dementia disease. Other people may perceive the person is functioning normally, especially if their interaction requires no decision-making challenges.

Frustration

As a person begins experiencing symptoms of dementia, she may be aware her mind is not responding the way it should. Words that used to flow easily become halting. Information that used to be readily available disappears. Directions to familiar places become illusive. Simple conversations with friends become jumbles of words that don't make sense. Even if she doesn't realize she's asked the same question or told the same story before, reactions on the faces of those who are listening tell it all. Nothing helps recall lost information, and her mind grows increasingly cloudy. People in these circumstances may become increasingly frustrated with themselves because they can't make things right, and often frustrated with others who can't help them.

Helplessness

Since dementia diseases are "question mark" diseases—full of unknowns—with inevitably poor outcomes, some people feel helpless and hopeless. Inability to stop changes occurring in actions and abilities leads to a helpless sense of losing control and self-determination. Since no cure—and few effective medicinal treatments—is available, some people living with dementia understandably feel like giving up and give in to self-isolation and withdrawal.

Fear

Whereas other diseases have symptoms and progressions that are more predictable and treatable, dementia progresses erratically and unpredictably. Living with the unknown is frightening and overwhelming for most people. It's hard to make plans when you don't know how you'll be affected or how long you'll need to live with the effects of an illness. This fear can be paralyzing, causing people to prematurely withdraw from society. They may withdraw because they don't see the point in engaging in a life that will become limiting, even if they don't know the timing of that limitation.

Anxiety

There are many uncertainties surrounding dementia diseases: Will it progress? How will it progress? Will I forget my family? Will I be a burden? Will I embarrass myself and others? These uncertainties can cause great anxiety; at the same time, the *certainty* of dementia diseases—no cures, memory and ability loss, eventual death—understandably cause anxiety as well. As someone living with dementia desperately tries to keep up with and understand conversations and continue to function as normally as possible, anxiety inevitably sets in. This is one of the most prevalent and powerful emotions people experience as they try to navigate dementia in the midst of life.

Anger

Understandably, some people are angry when they receive a diagnosis of a dementia disease. Anticipating how the disease will affect their lives—often by severely changing plans and limiting possibilities—can be devastating. Knowing that they are losing control of decision-making abilities and future self-determination causes anger. Sometimes this anger is misdirected toward the people who care for them instead of the disease that is causing the hardship. This is normal, and anger is part of the grieving process. Anger is often the outward expression of some of the other feelings already discussed such as confusion, frustration, fear, anxiety, and embarrassment.

Grief

Grief comes in many forms. Most people in today's society know about dementia diseases and their potential effects on a person's life. Knowledge that one has a dementia disease causes anticipatory grief as a person mourns the loss of memory to come and the difficulties that dementia will bring into life. People grieve the anticipated loss of things they had hoped to do or achieve, the anticipated burden they will place on their loved ones, the loss of precious time with family and friends. They grieve the future loss of independence.

Guilt

As mentioned above, it is not uncommon for people who receive a dementia diagnosis to feel guilt about the imposition and challenge they perceive they will become to family. Some may question their relationship with God, wondering what they did to deserve this fate, and feeling a sense of responsibility. As they deal with their grief, they anticipate dependency, which they believe will prevent people who will need to care for them from living as fully as they might have otherwise. They may not be able to hear assurances from family that caregiving will not be a burden.

When people receive a dementia diagnosis, they naturally experience questions and concerns unique to each person, as do their caregivers. Some are relieved to finally have a diagnosis for the memory loss and confusion they're experiencing. For some caregivers, a dementia diagnosis for their loved one validates what they've been suspecting and others couldn't see. But a diagnosis also causes much stress and anxiety. Many people living with or caring for those with dementia diseases also experience depression. Losing long-held roles that are important to those who live with dementia and those who offer caregiving is difficult. Both experience changes in self-determination, control, and a sense of purpose, all contributing to depression, which can be debilitating. Questions and concerns sometimes overwhelm people, including spiritually based questions.

SPIRITUAL CONCERNS AND QUESTIONS

While each person who suffers from dementia diseases will have different questions, just as they have varying emotions in response to a diagnosis, common themes emerge. The following questions, thoughts, and concerns frequently raised by those with dementia diseases can be helpful for us to consider and acknowledge when ministering to someone who has received such a diagnosis.

Guilt
- "I must have done something wrong to deserve this."
- "I hope my children can forgive me for the burden I will be to them."
- "I hope God forgive me for my anger and lack of trust."

Abandonment
- "God promised to be with me, but . . ."
- "God promised not to give me more than I can handle, but . . ."
- "I feel so isolated and alone. Even my faith community seems to have forgotten me."

Despair
- "There is no hope of my condition improving—why should I even try the many suggestions I'm told? Yet I'm supposed to trust God for everything."
- "Why should I go on living when I can no longer do anything for myself, much less anyone else?"

Ideally, people who have been active in faith communities will turn to their ministers for support and counsel when they receive a dementia disease diagnosis. Sometimes they don't, though, for fear their questions and concerns are signs of doubt or diminished faith. Sometimes they keep memory loss to themselves for fear of rejection and misunderstanding. As people experience these questions and concerns, they need someone to talk to, someone who will listen openly and nonjudgmentally.

Ministers, lay church leaders, friends, family, and caregivers are needed to address spiritual needs for:

Unconditional Love
Reassurance
Support
Encouragement
Trust
Acceptance
Inclusion
Hope

Keeping emotional and spiritual needs in mind while ministering to people with dementia diseases is essential. Some people express concerns openly, while others do not. We must be willing to walk with people wherever they are, being accepting, nonjudgmental, and confidential. If they want to talk, allow them the freedom to talk. If they don't want to talk, give them the freedom to be silent and support them with your presence and your prayers. Let them share whatever emotions they are feeling in the moment or not. As we realize that most people experiencing cognitive loss, and their caregivers, feel a jumble of often overwhelming emotions, it will enhance our sensitivity as we minister and enable us to show greater compassion. As we allow them to feel and be who they need to be, it helps them know that we can be a trusted partner. For people to confide some of their deepest feelings and spiritual doubts, they need to know that we are going to treat their trust sacredly.

Receiving a dementia disease diagnosis is the beginning of a long journey. It is imperative that no one walk this journey alone.

Chapter 4

IN THE BEGINNING:
EARLY STAGES OF DEMENTIA

Evelyn, who is seventy-two years old, is a pillar of her church and a well-respected woman in her community. Helping people and caring for her family motivates her. Gradually, though, she has begun to miss important birthdays, mix up ingredients for church meals, and repeat Bible lessons she's already taught. Evelyn has also begun to act impulsively, challenge people and refuse to turn over responsibilities she's no longer doing well. Her usually well-coifed hair is often mussed and her clothes are disheveled. She often has trouble finding the word she wants to use. As words begin to fail her and communication becomes more awkward, her church friends' and ministers' words begin to fail them, too. They want to help but don't know what to say or do to offer comfort and encouragement. They become afraid they'll say or do the wrong thing, causing her to get upset or agitated. So, they begin to say nothing.

Evelyn feels their slow disengagement like a dagger to her heart. In the confusion clouding her mind, though, she can't make things better. As a result, she slowly disengages from the church she has loved and served. People miss her, and some visit, but most eventually stop.

*E*velyn is just one example of someone in the early stages of dementia. Although no one's dementia disease progresses through the stages at the same rate or in the same way as another's, there are some generalities. In this chapter we'll discuss the early stages, which typically last about two to four years.

In the early stages of dementia diseases, the people living with the disease—and their caregivers—sometimes doubt the diagnosis and live in denial.

Remember early cell phones? Sometimes they worked and sometimes they didn't. When using an early cell phone, someone might be conversing on his phone and suddenly realize the person he was listening to was "gone." Just as suddenly, though, the person might be back in the conversation. Because of the phone's poor reception, the listener would have to play catch-up on the conversation. He might continue to listen once the connection was renewed, piecing together in his mind what must have been said during the "missing" parts. Responding when there are missing pieces can be tricky. Sometimes he might guess right and respond appropriately, but sometimes he would misunderstand and leave his caller wondering what he was talking about.

Like a cell phone with poor reception, in the early stages of dementia, message delivery in the brain is sometimes impeded and sometimes clear. Similarly, when someone has a dementia disease, sometimes she is on target with conversation and memories, and sometimes she is not. People in the early stages of dementia often miss parts of conversations, but they work hard to hide that fact. Understandably, they want to maintain the appearance of normalcy, and they often succeed. Because they succeed in the beginning, people who see and interact with them in social settings only often can't see the problems they're facing. Family members and caregivers, on the other hand, live with them and have many more occasions to see their inability to perform their usual tasks, make decisions, or carry on complex conversations.

COMMON INDICATORS OF DEMENTIA IN EARLY STAGES

In individuals struggling with the onset of dementia, there are many common indicators that may appear. Often the individual will brush them off as "not a big deal"—and indeed we all experience some of these as we age—but the occurrence of many of these indicators or repeated episodes of certain indicators may verify that someone is struggling with the onset of a dementia disease. Common signs include:

- Short-term memory loss
- Confusion
- Forgetting things
- Losing things
- Repeating questions and stories
- Word-finding difficulty
- Inappropriate mood swings
- Withdrawal
- Carelessness in actions and appearance
- Impatience with self and others
- Difficulty understanding and participating

When ministering to people in the early stages of dementia diseases, keep in mind the emotions they may be experiencing and spiritual concerns highlighted in the previous chapter. Being aware of those things heightens understanding and fosters compassionate responses to these signs and symptoms. Think about how confusing and frustrating it would be to know you are losing control. How would you respond—with anger, fear, withdrawal, despair? Be patient, and let God minister through you.

PRACTICAL WAYS TO MINISTER IN THE EARLY STAGES

When you suspect—or know—that one of your congregants is suffering from the early stages of a dementia disease, what can you do? There are many practical steps you can take to prepare yourself to adequately respond. They can all be summed up under one heading, however: Listen, listen, listen! Whether listening to the individual suffering, to those who know about dementia diseases, or to others in the community, by setting aside your preconceptions and fostering a willingness to listen, you will be better equipped to minster to and care for those suffering from dementia.

Educate yourself and your congregations about dementia diseases.

Contact your local Alzheimer's Association and find out what resources—trainings, support groups, materials—are available. Talk to people you've known who are caring for someone with dementia, denominational resource centers, and your Area Agency on Aging. Have a list of referrals readily available—good primary care doctors known for eldercare, home health caregivers, continuing care retirement communities, assisted living facilities, adult day care services, and more. Keep a running list.

Read books and articles on dementia, especially on spirituality and dementia. (See the list of resources for spiritual care and dementia at the end of this book.) Talk with church members who have lost loved ones with a dementia disease. Find out what was and was not helpful to them in terms of how their church responded to their needs.

Host a seminar for church and community members on understanding and establishing a power of attorney and advance directives. Conversations about future plans and wishes are essential for everyone, but they are especially needed when a family member is in the early stages of a dementia disease. Before he loses the capacity to make decisions for himself, find out his wishes for his care. Talk with him about who he wants to be responsible for making medical, financial, and legal decisions when he no longer can. Put these things in writing with his signature. If this is not done before he lacks the capacity to make important decisions, legal complications can ensue and difficult decisions will be even more difficult to make. Resources are offered at the back of this book.

Offer person-centered care.

Person-centered care considers the whole person, with his or her unique qualities, abilities, interests, preferences, and needs. Rather than focusing primarily on the disease with its medical needs and illness-related approaches, person-centered care looks first at the individual in a dignified and respectful manner, valuing him or her as a person.

It is very helpful to spend time getting to know the person you're visiting, building rapport. Learn what makes her uniquely her.

If the person you're visiting already has word-finding difficulty, talk with a family member or caregiver to discern information that will be helpful for you to know as you minister. Learning this information early into the process will help as time goes on and the person progresses further into dementia. Having truly paid attention, you will know the things you can do to help and to nurture their spirit.

Do a spiritual assessment.

A spiritual assessment is a tool to help you gather spiritual information about people you're visiting. When we go to a doctor's appointment or the hospital, one of the first things the nurse does before the doctor enters the room is collect medical background information and assess your physical needs. Likewise, a spiritual assessment enables you to discern faith background and spiritual needs of the person you're visiting. Information gathered can help you discover how to encourage her and help her practice her faith in ways that bring hope, purpose, peace and assurance of God's presence. The assessment helps you learn what aspects of her faith might give her strength to face what she's going through physically and emotionally.

While early information gathering is essential, this doesn't mean you should carry a clipboard with you on your visits and formally interview the person you're visiting. Instead, talk simply and naturally together as you spend time building a relationship. You can always start a conversation by sharing your own faith background and feelings about hope, purpose, and peace. Then, invite her to share. Weave this spiritual assessment into different conversations on different occasions so as not to overwhelm the person with questions all at once. Begin by asking her faith background questions like: Did she grow up going to church? If so, who did she go to church with? What does she enjoy the most about church? Here are more questions to consider.

What gives you hope? What gives you purpose?

Everyone needs to feel hope and a sense of purpose. Sadly, though, as dementia affects people, they lose the ability to initiate, much less understand, things that used to come easy. As their abilities wane, so does their self-esteem and sometimes sense of hope. Talk with the person you're visiting about what makes them feel hopeful. Caring and doing for others are essential aspects of a Christian's call and often give people a sense of hopefulness and purpose. Some people who lose the ability to help others become depressed. By learning what gives a person hope and purpose, we can create opportunities that allow her to use those gifts, perhaps in modified settings. In particular, doing ministry projects with her helps her contribute to others in need and provides a sense of purpose. Join with her to complete ministry projects that match her gifts and abilities.

Carl was always volunteering on weekends with Habitat for Humanity and doing projects around the church. His job as a construction foreman made him the perfect person to do these things, and he felt called to this ministry. But when confusion and short-term memory loss set in, he

could no longer keep up the pace at work or volunteering. He tinkered around, but he didn't accomplish much and began to feel depressed.

The minister asked Carl if he would come to volunteer when a younger church member who wanted to help out would also be there. This way he could mentor the young volunteer, showing him the ropes around the church. The younger volunteer listened thoughtfully to Carl and tactfully sought Carl's opinion as he proceeded to truly fix things. Gradually Carl's role shifted to assisting as he offered advice and supervision. He felt a real sense of pride and accomplishment as he nurtured several new volunteers for as long as he could. His hopefulness and sense of purpose returned as he began to feel that he was ministering as Christ would want him to.

Another example might be to help a congregant who used to create and give craft items to people, especially those who were sick. With supplies you purchase for her and gentle prompting to get her started, a congregant with dementia might be able to knit caps for babies like she used to. Or perhaps with your assistance, she might help you bake cookies and deliver them to a sick child. A lifelong, faithful person of prayer can continue to pray and praise from a printed list delivered weekly by a parishioner. A singer might participate in a choir with help from a fellow musician. The possibilities are endless.

Despite the advances of dementia, those living with the disease also desire to fulfill Christ's mandate in Matthew 25 to care for the sick, clothe the naked, provide hospitality to the stranger, visit the imprisoned, feed the hungry—just as we do.

What nurtures your spirit? Where and when do you feel closest to God?

As you begin addressing the needs of people with dementia, consider what makes them come alive, what provides them with comfort and peace. Is there common ground for sharing? Everyone feels God's presence in his or her life in a different way. By understanding these areas, you can better work with those with dementia to create opportunities allowing them to feel connected, comforted, and fulfilled. The following scenarios exemplify what makes some people feel closest to God.

Family and friends

Judith is a quiet woman of sixty-nine. As she begins to experience the effects of Alzheimer's disease, she's withdrawing further into herself. A devout Presbyterian, she's been active at her church, but no more. When asked what brings her comfort and helps her cope with life's transitions, she responds, "My family and friends." Knowing this, her family begins to take an even more active role in Judith's life, looking through family albums with her and reminiscing, spending more time with her, and assuring her of their love. Eventually, she goes to live with her daughter, surrounded by doting grandchildren. Her church friends, meanwhile, visit more often, supporting Judith and the family. They bring her to their homes for quiet family dinners where it doesn't matter if conversation is a little awkward at times. Judith enjoys listening to friendly conversation and fellowship.

Nature

Rachel suffers from crippling arthritis. Wheelchair bound, she's dependent for most of her physical care, and she has vascular dementia. She is becoming increasingly confused, and this confusion often expresses itself as anger toward caregivers at the assisted living facility where she lives. She often refuses care and emphatically asks people to leave her room. A church visitor has tried to visit with her, to offer spiritual support, but she refuses his visits until one beautiful spring day he asks her if she'd like to go outside. Her whole demeanor changes as she responds, "Yes." Once outside in the sunshine, the two don't talk, but listen to the birds and watch gentle breezes blowing through the trees. She seems transformed and becomes peaceful as being in nature makes her feel close to God.

Music

Grace was a renowned surgeon. At sixty-two she began showing signs of dementia and soon had to give up her practice. At sixty-five, she appears lost without her role of caring for others and sometimes lashes out as others try to care for her. In talking with her one day, her visitor discovers her love for opera. On the next visit she brings some music and listens to opera with

Grace. Immediately Grace's face transforms into an expression of bliss as she's transported into the unfolding story. Noticing this transformation, her caregivers initiate a music time each day. Gradually Grace begins to settle down and feel less agitated by her lack of control.

Being part of a faith community

The light streaming through her church's stained glass windows delights Nancy. At eighty years old, she's attended St. Mary's since she was born. Nancy never tires of hearing the organ swell or the choir sing, nor does she tire of serving coffee to visitors following the service. She feels God's presence strongly when she's there. But over the last few months she's felt people's stares when she tells a story or asks a question. She's just trying to socialize and take care of people, but they seem to be giving her weird looks and shying away when she comes close. Nancy knows she's felt confused lately and sometimes has trouble finding the right word to say. A longtime church friend notices Nancy's discomfort and awkwardness and reaches out to her. The friend buddies up with Nancy, sitting with her during worship services and taking walks in the sanctuary after hours to admire the windows and the beautiful pipe organ. Nancy regains her joy and confidence as the friend serves coffee alongside her and patiently models for others how to listen to the same story over and over and affirm Nancy for her gracious service.

Pets

Lucy had the friendliest golden retriever, Daisy. Everyone at church loved visiting with the inseparable pair. But eventually Daisy died, and Lucy, who had developed vascular dementia, soon went to live in an assisted living facility where she can't have pets. She seems lost and confused. The days drag on, until one day Lynne shows up with her pet therapy dog, Bumper. A golden retriever like Daisy, Bumper is effervescent and friendly. He gives Lucy kisses and sits adoringly at her feet as she rubs his head. Lucy cries with joy during every weekly visit and finally seems to feel more comfortable in her new home.

Children

Jack rarely comes out of his house now. As he's become more confused and disoriented, he's isolating himself and withdrawing, even from longtime friends. But when his granddaughter brings over her infant and toddler, he lights up. "My precious babies," he exclaims while holding the infant and watching the toddler run around. Church friends begin bringing small groups of children over to sing songs, tell Bible stories, and interact with Jack. Soon he accepts rides with a friend some Sundays to assist in the preschool room during church.

Art

Suzanne always volunteered to teach crafts at the local ministry center in town. Several times she went on mission trips with her church and enjoyed sharing her gift of making unique and beautiful things. Now that she has Alzheimer's, though, she never picks up her art supplies to draw, paint, or put anything together. In her mind's confusion, Suzanne can no longer initiate this activity that used to bring her, and others, such joy. Realizing this, a couple friends from her church begin visiting Suzanne, initiating a craft with her and assisting her as needed. They're amazed at how once they get her started, Suzanne is soon humming and chatting, showing them what to do. Over time, they bring a few other people with them and begin working in her sewing room on weekly projects for local charities. Suzanne is energized and engaged.

These are just a sampling of the many different ways a person might feel connected with God and with others. Consider what else might nurture someone's spirit. What nurtures you? When you identify these core longings in a person with Alzheimer's, you can begin to address their deepest needs, offering them connection and fulfillment that may have gone missing as their disease emerges.

What religious practices and symbols are important to you?

Many older people who have been lifelong churchgoers have been reading their Bibles, praying, and attending church for decades. These practices have become crucial ways in which they practice their faith. Worship, for them, may have included visual and sensory stimuli like looking at icons, crosses, crisp linens, and beautifully arranged flowers. They may feel God's presence as they smell incense, or hear God when the organ swells or the choir sings. Talk with the person you're visiting about religious practices and symbols that are important to her faith. As dementia progresses and people become unable to get to church, where they might experience and participate with these things, bring these things to them and perform these religious practices with them.

Provide frequent presence and conversation.

Spend time doing things that bring joy and comfort. As the individual you are visiting continues having memory lapses or other dementia-related challenges, it is important to be a consistent, faithful visitor. This will build up a trusting relationship over time. Eventually, she may not remember your name, but she will remember the feeling of comfort and acceptance she finds in your presence. On most days, she will welcome your visits. (There will be days when she may not be feeling well—physically or emotionally—and a visit won't be possible, or may be cut short. On the whole, however, your visits will be a welcome blessing.) As conversation becomes more difficult, stop relying on dialogue and spend time doing an activity with the person that you know she enjoys. Perhaps it's doing a puzzle, taking a walk, reading a story, planting flowers, even sitting and watching a favorite soap opera and then talking about it. Your presence with her and love for her is what is important. She may not be able to express it, but she will feel God's love through you.

Make church identification cards for people to carry in their wallets.

Some people who have dementia may not have family or friend caregivers to support them. They may be journeying down this path alone. In case of a medical or other crisis, they might not remember who needs to be called. To help alleviate such situations, the church should consider making cards for congregants suffering from dementia that simply say:

My name is _____

I am a member of St. Stephen's Episcopal Church at (address here)

Phone Number: _____

In case of an emergency, please call the church office and notify my minister.

The person with dementia can carry this in his wallet. Give the card to him in person, explaining that it will help the church be notified in case of an emergency. Watch him put it in his wallet. He may later forget it's there, much less who to call, but first responders will see it if there is an accident or sudden illness.

Show unconditional love and acceptance.

Visiting with and ministering to a person who has dementia can be challenging some days. She may say something inappropriate or critical. He may be feeling very frustrated and lash out at you angrily for no apparent reason. Perhaps one day, after weeks of really good visits, she refuses to look at you or speak to you. He may ask you the same question over and over, barely listening to your response.

We need to ask God to give us patience and understanding on the more difficult days. As Christians we must show the love of God to everyone. As Romans 8:38–39 reminds us, "For I am convinced that neither death, nor life, nor angels, nor rulers, nor things present, nor things to come, nor powers, nor height, nor depth, nor anything else in all creation will be able to separate us from the love of God in Christ Jesus our Lord" (NRSV). That includes dementia. We must be ambassadors of God's love, assuring people who are suffering that God loves them unconditionally and is always present. Offer yourself as a safe and loving person who will walk alongside the person living with dementia, and their caregiver, regardless of what they say or do.

Reminisce spiritually.

While reminiscing may seem difficult or impossible when memories are impaired, this can actually be an uplifting exercise with someone who is suffering from dementia. Short-term memory is predominantly affected with dementia disease, and people usually retain long-term memories far into their dementia. In order to encourage reminiscing, you can prompt memories with visual and sensual cues.

Pay attention to the church calendar and events in the life of the church. For example, at Easter time you could take gloves, a child's Easter bonnet, an Easter basket, a cross. Let your creative juices flow! Talk about the items with the person you're visiting and watch how they prompt memories of the season and its meaning.

Reminisce about family gatherings on Easter such as delicious Easter meals shared with family and friends. Remember special Easter worship services and rituals. Sing or play Easter songs such as "Christ the Lord Is Risen Today" or "Up from the Grave He Arose." Read an Easter-related scripture. Pray together, thanking God for the redeeming gift of his son, Jesus Christ, and God's love for the world.

Near All Saints' Day you could take along pictures of deceased relatives who were special to you. Talk about faith lessons you learned from your relatives. That may prompt the person you're visiting to share stories about her relatives. Sing or play "For All the Saints" with her. Pray, thanking God for people who taught you about God and asking Him to help you be faithful examples for future generations.

Find an old funeral home hand fan and take it with you on a visit. Many hand fans have Scripture verses on them or depict different religious scenes, such as Jesus standing and knocking at a door. Reminisce about how the fans might have been used in the past—at funerals, at old-time tent revivals that the person you are visiting may have attended in times gone by. See what memories are prompted. Sing or play a song related to the scene or Scripture on the fan.

Take a church bulletin and go through the service with them, reading scriptures, praying, singing or playing the hymns, summarizing the sermon. Carry offering envelopes and talk with them about giving to God and to others. This is a familiar item for faithful church members and can be used purely as a conversational start. Recall a time in your life when money was tight and giving hard, which might prompt them to remember a similar time in their lives. Reflect on how the faith community is there to help those in need. Be aware, however, that people with dementia perhaps are no longer able to make decisions about their finances and are considered vulnerable adults. Therefore, it is not ethical to ask for a contribution. Instead, should the parishioner offer to make a gift, simply thank them for the many gifts they have already given.

Reminisce with them about war times, the Great Depression, or other times of great challenge, and discuss how your faith helped you and your family through difficult situations. They may start spontaneously sharing about themselves. If not, ask if their faith helped them and their families through trying times, too. As you prompt them to respond to your stories, you may find that they have many of their own that they wish to tell.

Always go back to visit if you say you'll go back.

Sadly, people who are living with dementia are becoming too familiar with others disengaging from them. If you visit someone and it's not a good day or conversation is a little strained, don't let that keep you from returning another day. The next visit and the next will become easier as you get to know each other better and build a relationship. If you say you'll be back, don't use that as an excuse to leave, but rather use it as a real promise of continued fellowship. Ask for God's presence and guidance. The Holy Spirit will lead and support you, as Proverbs 3:5–6 says: "Trust in the LORD with all your heart, and lean not on your own understanding; in all your ways acknowledge Him, and He shall direct your paths."

Provide encouraging devotional literature.

There are devotional books specifically written for people with dementia (see the list of resources for spiritual care and dementia at the back of this book for suggestions). Have your church purchase a book for you to give the person you're visiting. On visits you could read a devotion together from a devotion book, which might prompt him to read when you're not there.

Always offer a blessing as you leave.

As you're leaving a visit, always offer an assurance of God's presence and love to the person you've been visiting. Look into her eyes and hold her hand or touch her arm as you offer a blessing, saying something like: "God bless you, Hope. It's been so nice visiting with you today. God loves you so much and so does our church. May you feel that love and God's presence with you every day."

People living with dementia are often struggling to stay connected to their normal lives. Losing important memories and experiencing more and more confusion is frightening and, at times, overwhelming. Hearing us speak words of reassurance is uplifting and can help sustain them on difficult days.

Chapter 5

AS TIME GOES ON:
MIDDLE STAGES OF DEMENTIA

*Paula moved in with her daughter, Vanessa, last year. At eighty-
four, she'd been living across town in her own home for fifty years until
dementia made it impossible for her to take care of herself. Sometimes
Paula enjoys listening to jazz music or watching her soap operas on TV,
but in the late afternoon she paces the halls and keeps going to the front
door like she's expecting someone to come home. Usually she enjoys meals,
which Vanessa prepares for the family, but lately she has been eating less
and picking off other people's plates. Paula used to enjoy helping Vanessa*

do household chores, but now she usually sits and stares out the window
while Vanessa works. Most of the time she seems content, but sometimes
she becomes angry or frustrated and even strikes out at Vanessa. Paula's
words, if she speaks, are often jumbled now, except when she and Vanessa
do their daily devotion together. Then, while quoting familiar Scripture
and singing old hymns, her words ring out clear and true.

*O*ne thing we must keep in mind as we minister to those with dementia diseases is that brain deterioration often causes changes in behavior and sometimes in personality. These changes are not something the individual living with a dementia disease can control. Some days may be clearer than other days, which can lead to thinking the person may have control over what's happening. She doesn't.

Barbara's mother, Irene, was always demanding, talkative, and
judgmental. Her strong personality pushed people away and even wore
on family members who wanted to be close to her. As Irene progressed
through the stages of Alzheimer's disease, though, she became sweeter
and sweeter. The harsh persona disappeared, and her family members
began to enjoy visits and outings with their "new" mother.

The type of personality shift Irene experienced—a softening of personality, greater warmth toward others—sometimes happens in people with dementia diseases. With others, it can go the opposite way—a happy, good-natured person becomes angry and sullen as dementia progresses. It all depends on what is being affected in the brain. We cannot expect that certain people will change in certain ways, or hold it against them if we find them changing in ways that we dislike.

It is important to emphasize, again, that dementia diseases affect each person uniquely. There are, however, some ways people are typically affected. As you seek to minister to people in the middle stages of dementia diseases—which can typically last from two to ten years—it is important to know some of these common effects on personality, physical abilities, and cognition so you can be more understanding and aware.

COMMON INDICATORS OF DEMENTIA IN MIDDLE STAGES

- Less vocal and/or speaks less intelligibly
- Less compliant
- More confused and lost
- More impulsive
- More disheveled in appearance
- Unable to recognize previously familiar people and places
- Suspicious
- Forgetful about what he or she has forgotten
- Making up stories to fill in memory gaps
- Paranoid, seeing or hearing things that aren't there
- Prone to wander
- Agitated by too much stimulation
- More comfortable in smaller environments
- In need of a predictable routine
- In need of cues and prompts
- Dependent on assistance with activities of daily life
- Experience "sun-downing"

Some people, especially in the middle stages of dementia, have a particularly difficult time in the late afternoon and early evening, a phenomenon that has come to be known as "sun-downing." At such times, they may become increasingly agitated or confused and prone to wander. A variety of things can contribute to this behavior, such as physical discomfort from pain, a noisy environment, or drug interaction. Most often the person is not able to identify the source of her discomfort.

Creating a calm environment with predictable activities and interactions helps. If you notice that someone you're visiting regularly experiences this late-afternoon difficulty, it might be best to plan morning visits. Too much stimulation can increase "sun-downing" behaviors. However, your visit could also have a calming effect of them, especially as you do things with them that you've learned brings them comfort. This is an area that might take some trial and error, and patience as you seek to understand "sun-downing" behavior.

COMMON EMOTIONAL CONCERNS

Emotional concerns highlighted in the previous chapters—confusion, anxiety, fear, frustration—continue into the middle stages of dementia diseases, and may become more intensified during these years.

Rose, an eighty-five-year-old woman with Alzheimer's disease, lives in the memory support unit of an assisted living facility. As she has progressed further into dementia, her anxiety and fear have intensified. Often, Rose sits in a chair crying and wringing her hands. She says how lost and alone she feels, even though other residents and staff are all around her. In her mind's confusion, she doesn't recognize her surroundings or the people she has been living around for the past three years. At this point, comfort to her would be the farmhouse she grew up in and her six siblings running around with her mom and dad nearby.

To help Rose feel less confused, staff keep a consistent routine of meals, activities, and resting time. They regularly offer her drinks, spend time talking with her, and hold her hand. They gently encourage her to attend activities they know she used to enjoy and some days still enjoys.

If you visit someone with emotional agitation similar to Rose, approach her with care and empathy. Even if you see her every week, introduce yourself quietly and tell her you're from her church. Remind her of the church's love and concern for her, and of your love. Ask if you can sit with her and hold her hand. After some quiet time comforting her and listening to her, you might say, "I know a scripture that helps me so much when I'm feeling sad. Psalm 23." Begin to recite it quietly. She will probably join in with you. You could continue by reading a devotion to her, or by singing an old hymn. Sometimes she may only be receptive to your presence and hand holding. Sometimes she may not be open to anything. Be flexible and understanding of however she's feeling.

While emotional concerns may increase as people progress further into the middle stages of dementia, this is not always the case. As time goes on, many begin to experience *decreased* feelings of embarrassment, denial, helplessness, grief and guilt. As memory loss increases, they may become less confused and anxious because they forget what they were anxious and confused about. Embarrassment may lessen as they become less aware of how they look and act. Being anxious and worrying about the future may decrease so they can live in the present, but this is not a given. Grief about losses they're experiencing, or will experience, may lessen. This does not, however, mean they don't still grieve past losses. Long-term memory lingers, and those losses may remain very painful.

If a person is no longer burdened with worry, anxiety, and fear, she may become more joyful and content. In such cases, this can be a more peaceful time for people living with a dementia disease. However, it can be a particularly trying time for loved ones. Memory loss in the late-middle stages may lessen anxiety for the person with dementia, but it also means the person has probably progressed to the point of not recognizing family and friends. Many family and friend caregivers experience pain and sorrow when mom, dad, spouse, sibling, or friend cannot recognize them and can no longer say their name. Be mindful of this pain as you minister to and offer support to caregivers.

As you minister to people in the middles stages of dementia, keep these spiritual needs in mind:

Unconditional Love
Reassurance
Support
Encouragement
Trust
Acceptance
Inclusion
Hope

You should keep employing ministries and practices high-lighted in the previous chapter, but you will also need to build upon these practices, adding tools that are specifically effective with people in the middle stages of dementia diseases. In the middle stages, people lose the ability to perform tasks that require higher levels of abstract thinking, sequencing, and mechanical ability. For example, they may have lost the ability or knowledge of how to turn on a CD player or radio without direction. Listening to music, which might soothe and comfort them, therefore becomes something they cannot initiate for themselves. They may have a Bible in their room, but can no longer remember what the Bible is for, much less know how to turn to a familiar passage that could give them hope, peace, and assurance of God's presence with them. So, among other kinds of ministry, more than ever people in the middle stages of dementia need us to initiate faith practices that we've come to learn are important to them.

PRACTICAL WAYS TO MINISTER IN THE MIDDLE STAGES

Visit more frequently, to build up trust and familiarity.

Although the person you're visiting may have progressed to a place of not recognizing you by name, he can recognize you as someone he likes, trusts, and with whom he is comfortable. In order to build up this familiarity, it will become important to provide more frequent visits. Visits don't need to be long. In fact, fifteen minutes or so is optimal. Sometimes the person you're visiting will make it obvious she wants or needs you to stay for a longer visit, or, by continuing to be anxious and agitated, she may indicate that she wants you to leave, shortening your visit. Pay attention to body language, and be flexible in how long you stay or how soon you leave.

Lead familiar religious rituals, and provide familiar religious symbols, to offer comfort and tap into memory.

Wear a cross or your clerical collar, if that's the norm for your denomination. These symbols automatically signal to the person with dementia that you represent your faith community. Seeing the cross, linens, candles, Bibles, and hymnals often initiates a sense of reverence. Find out which symbols and rituals are important to the person with whom you visit and provide them. Use familiar scriptures, prayers, and songs. As people lose the ability to grasp, use, and understand words, symbols of their faith speak to them.

Lucy could rarely put intelligible sentences together anymore, and spent much of her day anxiously pacing. It was difficult for her to sit still or follow simple instructions the nurses gave her when trying to get her up and ready for the day. Yet whenever her minister entered the memory support unit wearing a cross and carrying his Bible, she immediately would ask: "Is it time for church?" She would start singing "Jesus Loves Me," head for the area where she usually had worship time, and sit down. Seeing those religious symbols triggered deep faith memories and helped her access important faith expressions.

When people are in the middle stages of a dementia disease, they cannot learn new renditions of hymns, scriptures, or prayers. Now is the time they need to hear the traditional, older versions that they would have heard, sung, and repeated most of their lives. For people over seventy-five years of age, the King James Version of the Bible is most likely the version from which they memorized Scripture. Try to use this version when you read to them or recite verses. If you try to lead them in saying, for example, the Twenty-Third Psalm from Today's English Version of the Bible, they might look at you like you've desecrated something they consider sacred. If you try to lead them in singing an updated version of "Amazing Grace," you won't have participants. Stick to the tried and true.

As you provide familiar religious experiences, encourage as much participation as possible. Selecting well-known, traditional things they can say and do gives those in the middle stages of dementia a real sense of belonging and accomplishment when there are so many things they can no longer participate in fully. You'll see faces full of contentment and thankfulness as they're able to repeat and sing Scripture, songs, and prayers that have been integral parts of their faith. There are so many things people with more advanced dementia can still do and enjoy; they just can't initiate them.

Be a calming presence as a favorite activity is enjoyed.

As a person progresses further into dementia, she becomes less able to converse. Words may become halting, jumbled, confused, or hardly spoken. Speaking and answering questions become increasingly anxiety producing and overwhelming. So, make visits less reliant on talking. As you've gotten to know the person you're visiting, you know some of the activities she enjoys doing. Spend time doing an activity with her that she finds calming and enjoyable.

> *Mary's daytime routine involves a certain soap opera: "The Young and the Restless." If her visitor comes during show time, she won't be open to a visit. Instead, he visits at a different time, or sometimes he comes while the show is on and simply enjoys sitting with Mary on the couch, quietly watching her "story" unfold.*

You may wonder about the importance of doing something like watching TV or other non-faith-related activities with someone with dementia. Doing activities with them that they enjoy helps lay the groundwork for them to feel comfortable with you. On days when the person you visit is upset, feeling lonely, or anxious, your friendly presence might lift their spirits. They will be open to you during that more difficult time because they have grown to trust you. Because of the relationship you build as you spend valuable time just being with a parishioner with dementia, you may be able to have more consistent, "serious" visits doing faith-based activities, too.

Offer friendly narrative conversation instead of dialogue.

As conversation becomes more and more challenging for someone experiencing dementia, visitors need to be prepared to do more than converse. When we expect people who are having word-finding or word-delivery problems to enter into a conversation, we cause them to become anxious and overwhelmed. When they are having memory problems and we grill them with questions about what they've been doing or what they like to do, we set them up for failure and frustration. Instead, come to visit prepared with a couple of things you'll talk about—a recent trip, your grandkids, springtime, football, whatever you know would be of interest to that person. First, allow the person you're visiting to guide the visit as much as possible with what they want to say and do. Be prepared, though, to offer direction if the person can't. He will most likely enjoy your stories and enter in, when able, with comments, nods, or other facial expressions.

Appeal to the senses to prompt memories.

By appealing to various senses, you can help people access deep memories, which will often lead to unexpected participation. Consider some of the following sensory triggers.

Music

Cynthia, who is ninety-eight years old and in the late middle stages of dementia, usually sits silently in her wheelchair. She no longer initiates conversation and can rarely put two words together to respond to her family's simple questions. But when traditional hymns are played, it's like her entire body and mind awakens. She smiles with happiness while singing, fully engaged in the moment. When the music stops, she retreats back into herself.

Almost everyone enjoys some form of music. More significantly, as mentioned in the first chapter, approximately 75 percent of people over seventy-five years old claim religious connections are significant to them—and most religious traditions overwhelmingly contain some form of musical expression in worship. Music thus offers a powerful way for people to connect with their faith. Usually, playing traditional hymns with less orchestration and variation on the original tune is best for people with dementia. They recall the lyrics better when they can clearly hear them sung in the way they would have heard them while growing up in church. They also hear music better when it is sung and played in a lower register.

To shut out other distractions, and especially for hearing-impaired people, consider using headphones when playing music one-on-one with someone. Pay attention to her reaction to the headphones, though, as some people may not tolerate them well. (Earbuds are usually not well received, as they are not a familiar part of the person's past.)

Depending on your technical ability, you could create a playlist of favorite tunes for the person you're visiting. Or you may find a CD at the store that has all the hits from the era your parishioner grew up in. If the person can no longer tell you his favorites, consult with his caregivers. You can purchase a device that enables you to connect multiple headphones. Then, you can listen to what he is hearing and join along in the singing fun, too. You could also let caregivers listen along.

Let these experiences of listening and enjoying music with someone lead to thanking God together for the *gift of hearing*, one of God's blessings.

Tactile items
Providing items that people can touch and feel—things like stuffed sheep, dolls, sand, fabric, shells, hand tools, and the like—enhances memory stimulation. For example, "listening" to a large conch shell can prompt people to share memories of walks with family along the beach. Combing a doll's hair can recall memories of taking care of children. Feeling a soft, wooly stuffed sheep could remind someone of lambs frolicking in fields back home. Hand tools without sharp edges could prompt someone to think of past jobs or working with Dad on a project at home. The possibilities are endless.

Use shared tactile experiences with someone you're visiting to thank God with her for the *gift of touch*.

Picture books, calendars, or DVDs with scenery
Large picture books containing beautiful scenery, famous geographical landmarks, babies, animals, and events are good tools for sparking conversations with people who have dementia.

You probably receive free calendars in the mail from time to time. They often provide excellent visuals. Use calendar pages when visiting people with dementia to stimulate memories, which may be expressed or just momentarily remembered. Some calendars have Scripture verses written below the pictures. As you look at the calendar together, let the person you're visiting read the verses. Often, people in the middle stages of dementia diseases can no longer converse but still enjoy reading and feel a sense of accomplishment when they read.

Another option is to look for DVDs that show beautiful scenery as orchestral music is played. This appeals to two senses at once and will often hold the attention of a person with dementia. Watching such a video with them can provide restful, soothing moments of joy.

All of these visual stimuli can lead to a simple talk about the beauty of God's creation and our joy in caring for it. Take time to thank God for the *gift of sight*.

Aromas

Certain aromas can immediately conjure strong memories. Cinnamon may elicit memories of baking Christmas cookies or apple pie with Mom. Lavender may transport someone back to Grandmother's perfume or freshly laundered sheets hanging on a clothesline. Lemon zest could remind someone of lemonade stands on a hot summer day. Anise may prompt memories of licorice sticks purchased for a penny after school at the corner store. There are many options for the types of scented items you can bring. Be creative and try a variety.

See how memories may be sparked in people just from sniffing wonderful scents God created, and then talk about the *gift of smell* God gave us.

Food

Most people enjoy eating and find pleasure in eating with others. After speaking first with caregivers about any allergies, take a meal or snack to share with the person you'll be visiting. Eating an orange could lead to talking about visiting orange groves in Florida or California. Sharing an ice cream cone or ice pop might allow him to reminisce about ice-cream trucks that used to circle neighborhoods or sitting at the counter in the corner drug store. A piece of saltwater taffy could remind him of summertime trips to the beach or even pulling taffy. Then, pause to thank God for the *gift of taste.*

Serve Holy Communion.

Holy Communion is a sacred sacrament that many Christians now living with dementia have been receiving for decades. For many, it is a vital aspect of their faith expression. It reminds us of our sacred connection to God and of our redemption through the sacrifice of Jesus Christ. In the middle stages of dementia, though, a person may no longer attend worship at her church. Thus, if we don't take Holy Communion to her, she won't receive it. In many cases, her caregiver, who may be staying home with her, won't either. If possible, continue to offer this sacrament to people with the regularity they have historically been used to. As she watches you prepare the host and the cup, she will know what to do, and its meaning will spark her memories. When you see expressions of gratitude and holiness on her face, you will know how important it is to her. You will be reminded of its importance, too.

Become a pew companion or walking buddy.

In the middle stages of dementia, people have more difficulty participating in corporate worship. If attending church services has been a weekly faith practice for them, though, attendance is important. For as long as possible they need to feel the joy of worshipping God with fellow believers, and they benefit from the fellowship. We need to create a dementia-friendly, inclusive atmosphere in our churches so those with dementia diseases can participate, too.

Because of confusion in their mind and language difficulty, following a bulletin or singing from a hymnal may become impossible. People with dementia may impulsively speak out or ask questions. They may need to get up and wander a bit to release energy. In order to address these challenges, you might consider assigning a church member who has received training in understanding and communicating with people who have dementia diseases to sit with the person on Sunday mornings. The volunteer could help find hymns in the hymnal, scripture passages in the Bible, and parts of worship in the bulletin. He could quietly answer the person's questions or take a walk outside the sanctuary with the individual. The church could also supply some art supplies, magazines, or picture books for caregivers to give their loved one during the service, if diversions are needed.

Offer an alternative worship experience.

Sometimes those in the middle stages of dementia aren't able to attend corporate worship because of the need to wander, fidget, or talk impulsively. Caregivers may opt to stay at home with their loved one so as to not disrupt the service. This does not mean, however, that the church can't still provide opportunities for them to worship in other ways. How often, for example, do church sanctuaries sit unused during the week? One way to utilize this space is to invite a caregiver and the person she's caring for to come during the week for a brief devotion time in the sanctuary. Someone could play the piano for hymn-singing. You might schedule the time to coincide with the organist's or pianist's regular practice time, so the caregiver and person she's caring for could receive a mini-concert.

However, it is important that this time is specifically targeted for people with dementia who are no longer able to sit through a regular church service, and therefore adapted to their needs— shorter services, familiar hymns, and flexibility in how the time unfolds. The person experiencing dementia should be free to get up and wander, ask questions as needed, and just explore. Other family members or friends could attend, too. This might be a ministry you create for other caregivers in the community. In this way, those with dementia—and their caregivers—still have the joy of coming to the sanctuary to worship, even after regular services become too difficult.

Continue to educate your faith community in ways they can be compassionate.

In the past, Luther, a quiet and distinguished man of seventy-five, always dressed and groomed himself impeccably. A local retail business owner, he prided himself on excellent customer service and advice. Because of his strong work ethic and passion for his job, he continued to work beyond the normal retirement years. This is becoming a problem now, though, as memory loss is advancing and employees are finding it harder and harder to cover for him. He sometimes says unusual, unrelated things when addressing customers or leads them to the wrong part of the store to find items. At church, he seems confused and distracted when greeting people on Sundays and handing out bulletins in the sanctuary vestibule. His suits are looking wrinkled and shirts sometimes dirty. Quite often he forgets to wear a tie, and his hair sometimes looks like he's been through a wind tunnel. People are noticeably avoiding his door into the sanctuary and casting sideways glances at his unusual appearance. Luther feels their awkwardness and is embarrassed. He soon stops greeting people and sits alone in the balcony, waiting for the service to start. He's begun arriving late to work and his employees are at a loss for what to do to help him. They don't know what to say or do, since he is the boss.

At a time when Luther needs support and encouragement, he's beginning to feel ostracized. Two very important roles in his life—businessman and church greeter—are in jeopardy as memory loss compromises his ability perform them well. At first, people at work and church didn't realize what was going on with Luther until it reached the point where he could no longer function effectively. But, now that they realize it, could more compassionate responses be put into place?

Offering ongoing educational opportunities for people to learn about dementia and its effects will heighten understanding and elicit compassionate responses when people living with dementia are experiencing difficulties. When relating to Luther, a church friend might say, "Luther, the wind tossed your hair about a little before you came in. Let's step into the restroom and just straighten it a bit." Another church member could volunteer to subtly assist Luther as he greets congregants. As they provide caring assistance, they help him retain his dignity and retain an important act of service he performs at church. The church then needs to look further into how they can assist Luther, since it's obvious his memory loss must be impacting him in many other areas of his life. By talking with him and his family, church friends can discover information such as if he's eating well, able to take care of his home, could use assistance getting to doctors' visits, needs errands run, or would enjoy some companionship.

Always offer a blessing as you leave.

As with those in the early stages of dementia, the same is true here: always offer an assurance of God's presence and love to the person you've been visiting when you depart. Look into his eyes, hold his hand, or touch his arm as you offer words of blessing such as: "God bless you. It's been so nice visiting with you today. God loves you so much and so does our church. May you feel that love and God's presence with you every day."

Chapter 6

WHEN THE END IS IN SIGHT:
LATE STAGES OF DEMENTIA

Gayle and her sister, Anita, have been sitting by their mom's bed for a week. The doctor says she could die at any time, and they want to be there. Their ninety-three-year-old mother, Dotty, who is in the end stages of a fifteen-year battle with Alzheimer's disease, hasn't eaten in two weeks. She's battling pneumonia, too, and no one knows how she's hanging on, but she is.

As they sit in her room quietly talking, a CD of old traditional hymns, which their mom loves, plays. This isn't just any CD. It's a CD that Dotty's granddaughter, Rebecca, recorded for her. On it, Rebecca sings Dotty's five favorite hymns. Over and over the CD plays on a loop, until the daughters felt like pulling their hair out.

Finally, Gayle leans close to her mother's ear and says, "Mom, we've listened to Rebecca's CD for a long time now. We're going to put on some nice classical music for a while instead." Almost before Gayle finishes speaking, her mother's right arm raises and her hand waves back and forth, expressing her dislike of their idea. The daughters acquiesce, and the CD keeps playing. An hour and many verses of "Amazing Grace" later, Dotty quietly lets go.

o one can explain how or why Dotty clung on to life as she did. She'd been unable to really say what she was thinking or feeling for a few months. But despite appearing to be incoherent and "not there," she was clearly hearing what went on around her. Obviously, this sort of response is not always the case with people in the late stages of dementia diseases, but it does happen. People in the late stages of dementia can communicate through sighs, raised eyebrows, or movements of the hand, head, or eye. Be watching. It's better to err on the side of assuming that people are hearing and understanding what's going on around them, even if they can't respond vocally.

During the late stages of dementia, people receive the least visitors. A person can live for some time in this nominally responsive stage in which they need total care. Typically, the late stages of dementia last one to three years. Many people find this hard to see. For some, it makes them think of their own mortality or fear of dying. Sometimes people stop visiting because they just don't know what to do, or they may feel like they're wasting their time since the person doesn't respond to them. I've heard some visitors say, "It really won't matter that I came. She won't remember I was there, so what difference does it make?"

The truth is that it is not important whether our visit is remembered; these late-stage visits aren't about us. What's most important is that we are present with those who suffer, and that we live with them in the moment. Our job is simply to assure them of God's presence with them in that moment.

COMMON INDICATORS OF DEMENTIA IN LATE STAGES

- No longer recognizes family or self
- May put things in mouth and/or repeatedly caress things
- May only respond with "yes" or "no," nods or shakes of head, or become vocally unresponsive
- Totally dependent for all care
- Nonambulatory, spending all of their time in a wheelchair or bed
- Loses control of bowel and bladder
- Eventually loses ability to swallow

Jane, a ninety-one-year-old woman in the end stages of Alzheimer's disease, sits in a wheelchair during the day. She rarely opens her eyes and her head is usually drooped toward her chest. Most of the time her face looks peaceful, and she seems comfortable. Her hands lay in her lap, and Jane appears to be in her own world. Sometimes, when she's asked a question, Jane quietly responds, "Um-hum" or shakes her head to say no. If she does respond she usually answers appropriately to the question asked, but this occurs rarely, as does any form of emotion.

When the Twenty-Third Psalm is recited, though, things change. One day as Jane silently mouths many of the Scripture's words, a tear slowly makes its way down her cheek. When asked if saying the Scripture made her sad, she shakes her head. When asked if it brought her comfort, Jane says, "Um-hum." When asked if the Scripture made her think of God walking with her, Jane responds, "Um-hum," and a gentle smile spreads across her face.

EMOTIONAL CONCERNS

When people are in the end stages of a dementia disease, it's not always easy to tell what emotions they're feeling. Responses may be subtle, barely detectable, or seemingly not there at all. Caregivers and friends have to closely observe body language and sometimes guess what might be going on based on knowledge of past reactions in similar circumstances.

As we visit with those in the later stages, we should be careful to notice these subtle expressions. When you've gotten to know someone in the earlier stages of a dementia disease, you'll know better how she might respond to something in the late stages. Caregivers can also help interpret emotions being expressed. Tears in her eyes in response to a song she is listening to could indicate joy or sadness upon hearing the lyrics. A grimace in response to your touch could indicate fear or pain upon touch. Laughter can be a multifaceted emotional release or a happy reaction to something that is occurring. If you see a tearful response, try asking: "Are you in pain?" See if she can respond with "yes" or "no," or the shake or nod of her head. Do the same type of questioning if you suspect happiness, fear, sadness, or other emotions. Just as importantly, give them a chance to respond. We may not be able to know for sure what the underlying emotion is, but we must strive to remember that just because someone cannot express his feelings doesn't mean he's not feeling them. What's most important is that they feel your love and compassion as you're with them. Your presence will reassure and comfort them.

SPIRITUAL NEEDS

As life wanes and draws closer to its end, a person's physical, emotional, *and* spiritual needs become more basic. At this point he needs to feel surrounded by love. He needs to have people in whom he can put ultimate trust when it comes to caring for his needs and keeping him safe, since he can no longer do this for himself. And, most critically, he needs to be assured of God's presence and peace.

PRACTICAL WAYS TO MINISTER IN THE LATE STAGES

Live in the present moment with them.

Before entering the space in which a late-stage dementia patient resides, empty your mind of the day's distractions and clutter. Be fully present with her, sitting by her bedside or chair and focusing on her. As you sit there, you might look around her room and notice things. You can learn a lot about a person by looking around her room. Often, the items found there will be those that are most precious to her, as this is now the one room in which she predominantly resides. As you look at them, you might thank God for the trips, or friends, or family members they represent. Thank God for all the people who touched and blessed her life and whose lives she touched and blessed. Look at or hold her hand, feel the calluses or scars, and thank God for all the ways she served others and offered loving touches to them. Look at the wrinkles on her face and spend time thinking about and thanking God for all of the life experiences that put them there. Most importantly, spend time in prayer for her. Thank God for the gift she is to this world and the rest and peace she will enjoy with God in the next.

Be fully present.

Be a quiet, listening presence.

Introduce yourself quietly each time you visit, but don't feel that you have to continue to talk. Your presence with the person is the most important thing. You will not be listening to him talk, of course, because his words have failed at this point. So, become comfortable in the silence. Listen to the rhythm of his breathing and feel the presence of his spirit.

Provide gentle touch, if it is comforting for the person.

If the person you're visiting cannot say for herself, and if you haven't been able to build up a previous relationship, ask her caregiver if she likes to be touched. If you can get that information, always be respectful of her wishes. If you don't know, and can't find out, try gently touching her hand or touching her on the arm or shoulder. Observe her reaction carefully, though. As we've noted, even when a person is no longer talking and appears nonresponsive, facial expressions, shrugging, or moving away from your hand will indicate that either she's not comfortable with your touch or it hurts when you touch her. Be watching for these visual cues and comply with her nonverbal wishes.

Offer experiences that appeal to the senses.

If you haven't learned this information from previous visits, ask a person's caregiver about his allergies and likes or dislikes of lotion. If you find out he would enjoy this kind of touch, gently applying lotion to his hands or face can be very soothing and comforting. As emphasized in the middle stages, providing aromatherapy and smelling candles, incense, or spices can provide pleasure. If it is an activity he enjoys, you might take him outside for a walk in the sunshine or to sit under an awning and enjoy whatever weather is occurring. If going outside isn't an option, playing a DVD with beautiful seasonal pictures and soothing symphonic music might be comforting as well.

Provide quiet, familiar music.

As you sit with someone in the late stages of dementia, music can be particularly comforting. Find out from the family or caregiver what kind of music the person enjoys and play it. When she is near the end of life, though, is usually not the time to play John Philip Sousa marches or vigorous symphonic pieces. Rather, opt for quieter, gentler pieces. Then, sit with her, listening to the music together.

Read Scripture, or prayers from prayer books.

Elliott, a gentleman from Edinburgh, Scotland, came to live in the United States with his son and daughter-in-law when his wife died. Until attending her funeral, they had not realized he'd already begun to show signs of dementia. After living with them for several years, they recently moved him into a skilled care nursing center because he needed total care. For the last two weeks, he hadn't eaten or drunk anything. He was under hospice care now, and no one knew how he was still holding on.

When a church visitor arrived, Elliott's breathing was erratic, and he was nonresponsive. Sitting next to his bed, his visitor greeted him and offered to read to him from the Bible. The visitor knew, from talking with Elliott's son Micah, that the Bible had been a very important part of Elliott's faith journey. Turning to the Psalms, he started reading. After reading Psalm 42, the visitor looked over and noticed that Elliott's head on the pillow had inched closer while he was reading. As he read John 14, Elliott's head continued to move closer and closer. He still made no sound, except the sound of his breathing, which had gotten deeper and slower. When the visitor was done reading some Psalms, and after sitting with Elliott for a while, he quietly said the Lord's Prayer. Closing the book, he assured Elliott of his prayers and God's presence before leaving. Elliott died peacefully, forty-five minutes after his visitor left.

Was Elliott waiting to hear those sacred words of peace and closure? Only God knows for sure. But because of his head movement we know that he was listening and aware of the visitor's presence with him. Through the calming of his breathing we can tell that the prayers and the Psalms brought him some needed peace and relaxation. God used this visitor to minister to Elliott in a powerful way, even if Elliott couldn't "say" anything. Prayer books and scripture that have been an integral part of someone's life can have a profound effect upon people in later stages of dementia, offering peace and comfort that they might not find in any other way.

Value people for who they are, not what they can do.

Have you ever held a newborn baby? Pause to think about how it felt. Looking into the precious face of that newborn child is awe inspiring, isn't it? It's hard not to be emotionally overwhelmed as you study each tiny feature and feel her velvety-smooth skin. She is sheer perfection.

Now, consider: Can she do anything for you or for anyone? Obviously not, but of course, that doesn't matter. In those moments of adoration as you hold her, you are overwhelmed with joy and thankfulness because she *is*. She is a wonderful creation of God.

Consider the other end of life's spectrum, when you visit someone in the end stages of dementia. She's no longer able to do anything for herself, or anyone else, yet her value is just a great as that of a newborn child. We are all equally valuable in the eyes of God, but too often, when it comes to the end of someone's life, we fail to honor their true worth.

Our society predominantly values people for what they can say and what they can do. If we're not careful, we might buy into that type of thinking for ourselves and others. When we become frail and elderly, dependent on others for care and direction, society is quick to wonder why we are still hanging on. But Psalm 139:13–14 reminds us: "For You formed my inward parts; You covered me in my mother's womb. I will praise You, for I am fearfully and wonderfully made; marvelous are Your works, and that my soul knows very well." God walks with us through all the ups and downs in our lives and loves us for who he created us to be, not because of what we do.

This is the value we need to feel for ourselves and others. We are made in the image of God. We are valued because of who we are, not because of what we can do. So, when we look down into the beautiful face of someone in the end stages of dementia, let us thank God for that person and all that she *is*.

Always offer a blessing as you leave.

Whether the person is in early, middle, or late stages of dementia, this piece of practical ministry remains the same: always offer an assurance of God's presence and love to the person you've been visiting when you depart. Look into his eyes, hold his hand or touch his arm, and offer a blessing: "God bless you. It's been so nice visiting with you today. God loves you so much and so does our church. May you feel that love and God's presence with you every day."

Chapter 7

SO, WHAT DO I SAY?

*W*e have seen the ways dementia diseases typically progress and found that there are practical ways to minister
to people at each new stage. In this chapter, I'd like to dig a little
deeper to focus specifically on the act of communication. As you
visit people living with dementia, one of the greatest struggles you
may find is knowing what to say, how to say it, and how to express
some things without words.

Not knowing how to communicate with someone who is experiencing dementia is one of the main reasons people stop visiting. As a dementia disease progresses in someone we're visiting and her words begin to fail, learning new ways to communicate with her—and realizing that we communicate through more than words—is essential. A look, a touch, the tone of our voice, how we speak through our posture and gestures are all important aspects of communication. Silently sitting with someone and being fully present speaks volumes without speaking. Understanding how to communicate with people as they progress through dementia diseases is vitally important if we are to minister to them effectively.

COMMUNICATION IN THE BEGINNING

A person in the early stages of cognitive impairment may be able to speak without difficulty. The content of her speech becomes challenging, however, as short-term memory fails and stories and questions are repeated. If a story is repeated, listen and express interest in hearing it again. Telling her she's already told you the story five times just serves to embarrass and frustrate her. She honestly doesn't remember the previous telling.

The same is true for repeated questions. He truly doesn't remember asking the question or receiving your answer. Simply answering the question again, as if you're answering for the first time, is the best solution. Saying, "I already answered that question," humiliates the person you're conversing with. One way to help avoid repeated questions is to try writing down the answer to a frequently asked question as a reminder. For example: "Sue Smith will pick you up for church at 9:30 am on Sunday." If he asks the question again, you could show him the note and say, "Oh, here. She wrote it down for you to see." Then put that note in a prominent place. This does not mean he won't ask again, but having this visible reminder might help answer the question before it needs to be asked.

As her disease begins to progress, the person you're visiting may know what she wants to say but have difficulty getting the words out. Give her time to express herself. If it becomes obvious she can't get the words out and she's getting frustrated, acknowledge her frustration and try to lead the conversation down a different path. Often this relieves momentary tension.

The most important thing to remember is that physiological changes occurring in the brain are causing language difficulties. The person living with dementia is not capable of controlling his memory or communication lapses, but in the early stages he is often aware he is making mistakes he cannot control. As we keep this in mind, we can be motivated to respond out of love and with genuine compassion. If you fail to say the right thing, though, and inadvertently seem to cause further frustration, cut yourself some slack. Remind yourself that you are genuinely seeking to serve, in Christ's name, and try again. The person will feel and see your genuine concern.

COMMUNICATION TIPS FOR VISITING IN THE MIDDLE TO LATE STAGES

When you begin visiting someone in the middle or later stages of a dementia disease, the ways you've learned to communicate with people in the earlier stages may not work. Often, as we've seen, people in the middle stages have word-finding difficulty or may speak nonsensically. Their memory becomes so faulty that conversation may become impossible to hold with any consistency. In the late stages they will eventually not be able to speak at all. While it can feel hopeless to try and communicate, it simply takes time, patience, and a willingness to try a variety of approaches.

Each time you visit, approach from the front with a smile on your face, say hello, extend your hand, and introduce yourself.

Assume the person living with a dementia disease may not remember your name or why you're coming to see her, even if it's only been a week since your last visit. Have a smile on your face and look into her eyes. This will set a friendly tone and usually elicit a similar response from her.

If he is seated, get down on his level or below.

Standing over someone who is confused and experiencing dementia can create tension and a feeling of intimidation. Sitting with him enhances his comfort level with your presence. Sitting lower than him shows respect and helps him feel more in control.

Always greet them by their preferred name.

Out of respect, elders are often called Mr., Miss, or Mrs., and then their last name. But as dementia progresses in a person, she may no longer remember she's married. If this is the case, she may respond better to her given name. Pay attention to what is best for each individual, and adjust accordingly.

As much as possible, let them lead conversations.
Enter their reality, and go where they are.

Sometimes a person may get fixated on one thing. Go along with them. Some people living with dementia diseases make up stories to fill in gaps and to be part of the conversation. Again, go along with what they say. Don't correct them, even when you know the tales aren't true. It is their reality, and trying to force them to acknowledge something they cannot remember will only create agitation. Use their stories or comments to begin a conversation they can have an active part in.

For example:

> One day Sam is in a big hurry when you arrive to see him. "I can't visit today," he says, "I have to pack my suitcase and get ready for my trip." When you ask where he's going, he responds, "I've been named National Baseball Commissioner and have to get to an important meeting for my job." At ninety-seven, Sam's obviously too old for that responsibility, but he believes the job is his. He's obviously very excited by it.

In such a circumstance, it is best not to negate a person's excitement or try to bring him back to reality. Instead, you could try: "That's so exciting, Sam. What an honor! I love baseball, too. What's your favorite team?" Or, "I played little league when I was a kid; did you?" "Do you have a favorite position on the team?" "Have you ever hit a home run?"

In other words, pick up the ball and run with it, metaphorically speaking. As you join Sam in his reality, he'll enjoy the conversation, and there is a good chance he'll soon move away from his fixation on packing as he reminisces about his favorite game. You'll be able to have a good visit with him as he becomes an active participant in a conversation he really enjoys. You'll get to know more about him and have talking points for future conversations.

Or consider an alternative situation:

> Sometimes when you visit Hilda, you find her pacing anxiously and wringing her hands as she waits impatiently for her mother to arrive. Hilda, who's ninety-two, has long since forgotten that her mom died thirty years ago. She wants her mother. When you arrive to visit with her, she tells you she can't visit today, she's waiting for her mother to arrive for a visit and doesn't want to miss her.

In such cases, you might try saying something like: "You know, I bet your mom's a wonderful lady. It sounds like you love her very much. Is she a good cook like my mom?" See if you can engage Hilda in reminiscing about her mother. Before long you may be able to sit down with her and shift gears to talk about advice you got from your mother. As you reflect on advice your mom gave you like, "If you don't have something nice to say, _____," see if Hilda can fill in the blank. Shift gears again and talk about advice Hilda gives her children, or her nieces and nephews. Before you know it, her thoughts will be going down a new path that she will enjoy walking with you.

Try taking the word "remember" out of your vocabulary.

This is no easy feat. We spend lots of time remembering and telling our life stories to one another. Memory loss robs us of memories that remind us of who we are. It's especially hard for family members when their loved one can no longer remember cherished events they've shared. Our impulse is to encourage those with dementia to try and remember such events. Yet in reality, because of the effects of dementia on their brain, they simply cannot. To push them to do so will only cause frustration, confusion, or embarrassment.

Even if they can no longer articulate memories, however, you can help those with dementia experience the joy and significance of events. For example, as you look at old photo albums, be prepared to talk about things you observe in the pictures: how happy or busy people look, the beauty or starkness of the scenery. Don't grill the person about who is in the pictures or specifics about the event; let them volunteer information if it comes into their memory.

Be prepared for your conversation to be more one-sided, with less dialogue.

You'll do most of the talking as a person progresses into her dementia disease, but as stated above, you should allow her to direct the conversation as much as possible. Come prepared with a few talking points when you visit. This relieves people with dementia from the pressure of trying to chitchat or think of responses that don't come easily. They'll enjoy your stories and memories. You may notice them nodding or shaking their head, laughing or sighing as they remember similar stories from their past as you talk. They may not be able to have conversation about themselves and what they did, but they still have memories and emotions that your stories help them recall. Or, they may just enjoy your enthusiasm and your story.

Use simple sentences.

When you speak with people in later stages of dementia, keep sentences short and concise. Allow the person time to process the idea being presented. Be patient for her response. Don't try to put words in her mouth to fill in the awkward silence, unless she wants you to try to guess the word she's having difficulty saying. To determine this, observe her body language. You should be able to tell her openness to your word-finding help. Likewise, you should be able to sense her frustration if you try to complete a thought. Keeping communication simple should help avoid these difficult situations.

Avoid asking a lot of questions.

When we come into a visit asking a lot of questions, the person we're visiting may feel like he's being interrogated. He may become anxious and withdrawn. As we noted, prompting him to remember things he can't remember is very challenging and frustrating. Additionally, he may not know how to respond, even if the question seems simple to you. The dementia may be affecting not only his ability to hear and comprehend what you are asking, but also his ability to form appropriate responses.

Do not argue. You will not win, and frustration will only increase—on both sides.

As has been pointed out before, people who are living with dementia are experiencing their own reality, which is quite different from what's actually happening in the world. Couple this with the fact that they are losing so much control, and that in the early and middle stages they are often aware of this loss, and you'll see heightened anxiety that can easily slide into frustration or anger. They truly believe what they are feeling, seeing, and experiencing is real. You will not be able to convince them otherwise, and they will not give in. Trying to bring them to your understanding of what is really happening will only escalate arguments, anxiety, and anger— something we want to avoid whenever possible.

Jim, a seventy-eight-year-old man with Parkinson's-related dementia, loves animals. When pet therapy dogs come to visit, his eyes light up and his hands automatically reach out to stroke them. So his visitor, Katie, decided to take him to the SPCA one day to see and pet the dogs. She thought she'd found the perfect activity to make Jim happy. However, to get him to the car, they first had to go through the memory support unit's locked doors, which he usually can't go beyond. As Katie held the door open for Jim to go through, he stopped and wouldn't budge. Instead of moving, he told her in no uncertain terms that he was not going through the door.

"OK," she said, "we'll just wait here a minute." Standing by his side she silently counted to ten and then enthusiastically said, "Let's go see some dogs, Jim. You're going to love it!" Without hesitation Jim began to walk with Katie. "OK!" he exclaimed excitedly.

Be forewarned: This tactic of stopping and waiting doesn't always work. Sometimes the person's mind is made up and no matter what you do, you will not succeed in getting him to do what you ask. But if you argue with him initially and say, "Oh, come on, Jim, you know you want to see the dogs," you probably wouldn't have a good outcome. Those with dementia don't recognize the irrationality of some of their behaviors, and they do not want to be argued with. However, in this instance something about waiting a few seconds and then reintroducing the idea enthusiastically got Jim's attention and helped him shift gears. On other days you'll have to try other approaches, and you may not succeed in getting the person to do what you'd like. Be creative.

Watch body language and facial expressions, for change in affect.

Only 7 percent of true communication occurs through words. Approximately 93 percent of communication happens through facial expressions, body language, voice tone, and inflection. Be aware that people with dementia are communicating with more than words, and so are you. For example, if you visit someone and your arms are crossed, he may assume you're angry. If your foot continually taps, he may assume you're nervous or anxious to leave. If you continually look around while visiting and don't focus on the person's eyes, he may begin to be nervous and restless.

Watch body language so you'll know when it's a good time for your visit to be over—both their body language and yours. Are they squirmy, looking around, anxious, or preoccupied? Do you find yourself focusing on other things besides the person you are visiting? Is your mind wandering aimlessly to other responsibilities for the day? If so, it's time for the visit to end. Know your limits, too. If you're feeling uncomfortable and ready to leave, they'll pick up on your body language and mirror it. A visit does not have to be lengthy to be a good visit.

Pay attention to the emotions behind the words.

Listen closely for the emotional feelings being expressed. Even if words are jumbled or nonsensical, listen to the emotion under the words. Mirror those emotions, words and sounds as you respond. Try repeating whatever sounds they are making. Reply, "Really?" Or, if you sense heightened emotions from them, perhaps, "Really!" This will show you're connected and listening to the person with dementia, and he will probably respond with engagement because he feels heard.

Assume they understand more than they can say.

Remember the story of Dotty from Chapter 6? Her family sat by her bedside as she was non-responsive near the end of her life. Yet when Dotty's daughter told her she was changing the CD of her granddaughter singing, Dotty signaled not to do it by lifting her arm. The family was shocked. They thought she was so near death that she couldn't hear or understand what they were saying, much less the songs that had been playing over and over. But Dotty was listening.

Likewise, do not talk about the person in her presence like she's not there. Always err on the side that she's hearing whatever you say.

Stay calm. Remember the duck.

If you are anxious and worried about what you'll say or do while visiting someone with dementia and you carry those feelings into your visit, there's a good chance the person you're visiting will become anxious and worried, too. You're preparing yourself through reading this book and doing other things to understand dementia and how to minister to people experiencing it. As you seek to serve in Christ's name, you will feel the presence of God with you to empower you. Be confident in your preparation.

Have you ever seen a duck gliding across a pond? It moves so gracefully, as though the glide requires no effort at all. Yet in order for that smoothness of movement to occur above the surface, what's happening underneath the water? The duck's feet are paddling furiously. When you're visiting someone with dementia, be a calm, non-anxious presence. Don't let him see your frustrations and fears under the surface. Present a calm demeanor, and there's a good chance he will mirror your calmness.

Chapter 8

WHO'S CARING FOR
THE CAREGIVERS?

Vanessa wants to keep bringing her mother to church. After all, she's been a member for fifty years. During that time her mom has done many things, like teach Sunday school, coordinate hospitality, lead women's circle groups, and perform a variety of other jobs. But lately her mom, Elizabeth, has been receiving disapproving looks at church, especially when she says something impulsive at an inappropriate time. Since being diagnosed with Lewy body dementia three years ago, Vanessa's usually mild-mannered mom has become more confused, and she sometimes hallucinates. Vanessa sees people shying away from them when they walk into rooms and feels people's awkwardness when they try to initiate conversation.

Deterred by this unwelcoming atmosphere, Vanessa begins staying home with Elizabeth, watching church on TV. They both miss their faith community and worshipping in their church. They miss having opportunities to serve others and study the Bible. But Vanessa is embarrassed for her mom, and she doesn't want people looking down on her. Even though Vanessa feels isolated, she feels she has no choice.

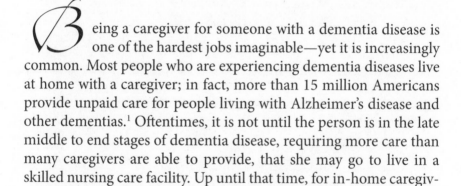

eing a caregiver for someone with a dementia disease is one of the hardest jobs imaginable—yet it is increasingly common. Most people who are experiencing dementia diseases live at home with a caregiver; in fact, more than 15 million Americans provide unpaid care for people living with Alzheimer's disease and other dementias.[1] Oftentimes, it is not until the person is in the late middle to end stages of dementia disease, requiring more care than many caregivers are able to provide, that she may go to live in a skilled nursing care facility. Up until that time, for in-home caregivers, caregiving is a 24/7 job.

While caregiving can be a physically demanding job, it is especially a very emotionally demanding one. Most caregivers, whether family, friend, or professional, feel a real sense of commitment to the person they are caring for. It is so much more than just a duty. Many caregivers are caring for someone they have journeyed through life with, whether mother, father, spouse, other relative, or lifelong friend. At other times during their life's journey together, the one they are caring for may have cared for them.

WHO ARE THE CAREGIVERS IN THE UNITED STATES?

According to the Alzheimer's Association, approximately two-thirds of caregivers in the United States. are women, and 34 percent are age sixty-five or older. More than two-thirds of caregivers are non-Hispanic white, while ten percent are African-American, eight percent are Hispanic, and five percent are Asian.[2]

The vast majority (85 percent) of unpaid care provided to older adults in the United States comes from family members, and more than half of primary caregivers of people with dementia take care of parents. Most caregivers either live with the care recipient or within twenty minutes of the care recipient. It is also estimated that 250,000 children and young adults between ages eight and eighteen provide help to someone with Alzheimer's disease or another dementia.[3]

The time and money of such care really adds up: In 2018, caregivers of people with Alzheimer's and other dementias provided an estimated 18.4 billion hours of unpaid assistance, a contribution to the nation valued at $232 billion—nearly eight times the total revenue of McDonald's in 2013. This is a staggering number, and one that highlights the many demands put on caregivers, typically without any monetary compensation in return. In fact, the value of informal care (not including caregivers' out-of-pocket costs) was nearly equal to the costs of direct medical and long-term care of dementia.[4]

Caregiving is strenuous, emotionally challenging work with little financial incentive. So why do people do it? The three primary reasons caregivers decide to provide care and assistance to a person with Alzheimer's disease, according to the Alzheimer's Association, are: the desire to keep a family member/friend at home (65 percent); the desire for proximity to the person with dementia (48 percent); and the caregiver's perceived obligation as a spouse or partner (38 percent).[5]

CHALLENGES FACING CAREGIVERS

Despite the demands caregiving requires, many caregivers are reluctant to ask for help or say they need anything when asked. Caregivers often feel they must do the caregiving themselves, especially spouses in long-term relationships. They feel it is their responsibility and commitment to care for their ailing husband or wife. For many, caregiving is a role they treasure. It gives them purpose. So, even when the demands of caregiving begin compromising caregivers' physical and emotional health, many will be hesitant to accept help or heed advice to take care of themselves.

The longer a caregiver cares for someone, the stronger the bond with and dependency from the person she's caring for may be. Understandably, the more the person she's caring for becomes dependent on just her, the harder it is for a visitor, or even other family members, to assist the person living with dementia. This is why it takes a slow and consistent presence to build up trust with the caregiver and the one she's caring for.

The responsibilities are daunting: physician appointments, listening, preparing meals, answering questions, comforting, guiding, dressing, bathing, and feeding—to name just a few. The list goes on and on. And while caregivers often express great satisfaction in being caregivers, they also express significant stress and feelings of isolation. The financial, physical, and emotional toll on caregivers is sometimes overwhelming. They lament over such things as not being able to go to church and feeling isolated from former activities. Some are sad or depressed as they watch a loved one decline. They may feel overworked or exhausted from lack of adequate sleep. They may become worn down from having to be constantly available to their loved one. As pastoral workers, we must keep offering to help and keep being proactive, finding ways to help when caregivers in our communities can't or won't ask.

PROVIDING PRACTICAL MINISTRY

Be a faithful and consistent support.

Because dementia diseases, especially Alzheimer's, can affect people for eight to twenty years, being a caregiver is a long-term commitment. Caregivers need people who can walk with them throughout the course of the disease, offering physical, emotional, and spiritual support. Sadly, though, caregivers are often forgotten. The old adage, "Out of sight . . . out of mind," definitely seems to apply to this demographic. As the caregiver starts staying home with her loved one, she eventually slips off the radar of most churches. When this happens, she doesn't get the compassionate care she so desperately needs.

As emphasized before, churches benefit from establishing a team approach to doing pastoral care. Teams who receive valuable dementia care training can be more alert to discovering people who may be in need of care in your church or community. To build trust and rapport, both people experiencing memory loss *and their caregivers* need faithful visitors. Some people on the team might coordinate taking care of tangible needs—repairs, yard work, shopping, rides to the doctor. Other volunteers can primarily care for emotional and spiritual needs, paying attention to both the person with dementia and the caregiver. Of course, these are big tasks. Rather than relying on one or two people to do everything, which can often lead to burnout, a team can minister interchangeably and flexibly.

Show respect and love for the caregiver's loved one.

Caregivers carefully guard the dignity of the person they love. They need to see that you truly respect and want to honor the person they love, even if you make mistakes while trying to do it. Because people with dementia are often stigmatized, caregivers strive to protect the one they're caring for from disrespect or public scrutiny. So, when a caregiver sees and feels meaningful interaction occur between her loved one and a visitor, she will likely respond with gratitude and appreciation, and encourage such interaction to continue.

When you visit, it is important to talk with the caregiver, offering them conversation and connection and checking in on their physical and emotional state. However, be sure you talk with the person who has dementia, too. Don't just talk around her or over her to the caregiver only. Compassionate visitors who show love and respect to the person they're caring for often help caregivers become more accepting of assistance and nurturing.

Recognize and accept caregivers' feelings and emotions. Be nonjudgmental and confidential.

Caregivers need people who will allow them to voice their tragedies and triumphs, their stresses and blessings. As visitors listen with open hearts and open minds, caregivers feel validated and valued. Sometimes they need someone to listen as they reminisce about the ways things used to be and the daily losses they're experiencing. Other times, caregivers need someone to hear how the act of serving and loving the person they are caring for is a blessing. They need sensitive, nonjudgmental visitors who can listen and then hold what's said to them with the utmost respect and confidentiality. Caregivers don't need or expect us to solve all of their problems, because we can't. Rather than thinking about how we can solve their problems the whole time they are talking, we need to just *listen, listen, listen.*

Encourage caregivers to get a second opinion, if needed.

Sometimes a doctor may not understand or see the scope of memory loss that a person and his caregivers are dealing with. If the caregivers or the person experiencing memory loss feel they are not being adequately heard, encourage them to seek a second opinion. Likewise, if their loved one receives a dementia diagnosis and caregivers simply can't see it (whether because of denial, disbelief, or unanswered questions), encourage a second opinion for clarification.

Facilitate a family meeting with adult children.

Sometimes families experience difficulty talking, listening, and truly hearing one another when a loved one is experiencing decline due to dementia. It is not uncommon for one family member to shoulder most of the caregiving responsibility. This can cause frustration and resentment to build up toward other family members who nominally share in providing care. Sometimes out-of-town children are shocked when they return home after extended absences to find Mom or Dad significantly changed from the last time they visited. Although the in-town sibling may have been communicating the parent's decline, seeing the changes in a person is often a rude awakening. Then, feelings of disbelief or unrealistic expectations of care from siblings can leave the day-to-day caregiver feeling wounded and overwhelmed. Sometimes families need a meeting, with all concerned people present, in a safe, neutral space with an objective listener.

To enhance communication, planning and responsibility sharing, the family minister could offer to facilitate a family discussion. Better understanding and cooperation may follow as people get on the same page. Sometimes people don't see what they could be doing to help, or sometimes they don't see the huge burden of care one sibling is bearing. Having a family meeting can be very insightful and help bring reconciliation and cooperation.

Offer Holy Communion and a short worship time.

As a caregiver begins staying home more and more with her loved one, she misses out on worshiping in her faith community with fellow parishioners, too. A minister or lay minister could offer Holy Communion and a brief worship time with the caregiver and her loved one. Sharing in this holy sacrament can be very meaningful for everyone as it meets important spiritual needs.

Go with caregivers to doctor appointments and be a friendly presence.

As he has progressed further into Alzheimer's disease, Claude hates going to the doctor. Getting him dressed and ready to leave is a struggle of wills that leaves his wife, Sara, exhausted. Getting him to the car and successfully buckled in takes diplomacy and cunning, much less trying to get the car started and going before Claude tries to get out. Sara is used to doing everything for Claude herself, but she realizes she needs help. She calls their church.

Having a volunteer drive a caregiver and loved one to an appointment, drop them off at the door, park and then come and offer companionship in the waiting area can make a stressful outing much less so. As the volunteer builds a relationship with Claude, he'll be able to offer valuable assistance just by being present. Sara can register and take care of business while Claude is companionably cared for. As Sara becomes more comfortable seeking and receiving help, she'll feel less overwhelmed and alone. This may enable her to trust church visitors to walk with Claude and her in other areas of their journey, providing important emotional and spiritual support in addition to helping with basic needs.

Anticipate caregivers' needs, and look beyond their "Fines."

How often do we greet someone with an offhanded, "How're you doing?" Before they've answered, we've passed one another and keep walking as the person responds: "Fine. You?" It's not that we don't care; these kinds of greetings are just social habit. But what would it look like to really take time to hear, much less see, how the other person is doing?

People who are caring for loved ones with dementia diseases are often struggling under the weight of so many responsibilities. Yet rarely in our society do we simply admit to how we're really feeling. This can be particularly true of caregivers, who may feel that other people don't really want to know how they're feeling or that even if they do, they can't really help. They may believe that caregiving is their responsibility, and that they don't need to burden anyone else with their problems. Meanwhile, they're exhausted and sometimes overwhelmed.

How can we step into this space and offer support? The first thing is to look beyond their "Fines" or pat answers when we inquire about their well-being. Taking time to observe a person's posture, eyes, or voice can help you see and feel his fatigue. If you notice these things, a follow-up call offering support and care might encourage him to acknowledge some of the strain he's feeling. If the caregiver is not open to a visit or assistance when you call, don't give up. Try again another day. Send an encouraging card. Call when you're at the grocery store one day and offer to pick up needed items. Take a casserole or some fresh flowers to their home. Be creative, looking for ways to gently offer encouragement or care to those who might be reluctant to ask for it.

Meet tangible needs.

Often a first response to a church member's illness is providing a casserole. This is a vital ministry, but it is a beginning point. Again, dementia diseases are usually long term, and caregivers are often hesitant to ask for help. Potential visitors need to be proactive. While getting to know the family, find out their likes and dislikes, including allergies or favorite foods, activities that bring joy, and needs that might have fallen to the wayside. Be observant.

Perhaps you learn that the caregiver is an avid gardener, yet you've noticed that her flowerbeds are getting weedy. Show up one day with gloves on and gardening tools, ready to go to work. Rake leaves in the fall. Cut grass in the summer. Plant flowers in the spring.

Perhaps you notice the caregiver might need a ramp built onto her home to accommodate her loved one's unsteady gait or difficulty climbing steps. Offer to build one, get lumber donated, and enlist volunteers. There are many such projects that can make a dramatic and tangible difference in the life of a caregiver and the person in her care; it simply takes observation and initiative on our part to step in and offer to do something about it.

Offer respite.

After you've built up a trusting relationship with a person living with dementia, you might be able to offer some much-needed respite care. Perhaps the caregiver will feel free to join a friend for dinner, go to a movie, or attend on important social function while you stay at home with her loved one. It's also possible that the caregiver may not feel comfortable leaving home. In that case, offer in-home respite. This could allow the caregiver to go into another room to read, nap, pursue a hobby, or do other things. She'll be able to enjoy a break but will still be "on site" should her loved one need her immediate assistance.

Host a dinner at your home.

Hosting a dinner at your home for a caregiver and his loved one with dementia can provide a good opportunity for them to enjoy others' company in a non-threatening, nonjudgmental environment. Rather than inviting the extended family to attend, consider limiting it to just one or two other people. Keep things simple. The environment should be warm, inviting, and low-key. Prepare food and drink that you've learned are favorites. Think ahead about music you might play, walks you might take, topics you might talk about over dinner. Enjoy one another's company as you do at any dinner party you host.

Be available to discuss important options and support individual needs.

Caring for someone who has a dementia disease is physically, emotionally, and spiritually taxing. Over time the caregiver's health may become compromised. As the needs of a caregiver's loved one progress, her ability to care for him may become too challenging. Decisions may need to be made about whether it's time for the family to find a place for their loved one in a memory support center.

As you've built up a relationship with the caregiver and her loved one, she might process some of these thoughts with you or need to process them with your church's minister. Conversations with a caregiver going through this discernment process require diplomacy. Listening is the key, rather than telling her what to do or offering unsolicited advice.

If you've been visiting a caregiver over a period of time and have observed her fatigue or decline, it may be time for the minister or a trained counselor to visit and initiate a needed conversation. The caregiver may not raise concerns but might need to be encouraged to do so for her physical, emotional, and spiritual health. The minister can then gently guide the conversation.

Placing her loved one in a memory support center may be a time of great opportunity for the caregiver. As she begins to process the need for help, and as she actually begins receiving it, much-needed relief can follow as she feels less overwhelmed. The caregiver may also feel less burdened when she sees that her loved one is receiving good care in an environment dedicated to dementia care.

Considering an alternate living option for a loved one with dementia can be a very healthy step. While discussing the pros and cons with someone, you might encourage her to consider that surrounding her loved one with people who are trained and able to care for him on a daily basis in a safe and stimulating environment is a loving and viable option. It allows their relationship to move from caregiver back to spouse, daughter, son.

Today, many specialized living opportunities exist for those with dementia, ranging from memory care units that are part of larger continuing care retirement communities to smaller assisted living facilities focused on dementia care. Because there are growing options in many communities, it is often possible to compare and choose while making this very important decision. Resources listed at the back of this book are available to help evaluate these options.

Reputable organizations are happy to meet with caregivers, loved ones, and the potential resident. As you've built a relationship with the family, they may ask you to visit some facilities with them. If this is the case, when you tour such facilities, encourage the family to note the condition of the buildings and grounds. Notice how care providers interact with residents. Do they make eye contact with the loved one? Do they convey a sense of caring?

Encourage the caregiver to ask questions of various people and the facilities. Some questions to consider include:

- Is the organization's accreditation and inspection current? (Ask to see licenses.)
- How are the organization's finances?
- What are the qualifications of key personnel such as the Executive Director, the Chief Financial Officer, and the Director of Nursing? How long have they worked for this organization?
- What are the ratios of direct care staff to residents? (Compare the answer to required levels in your state and other organizations.)
- Do residents receive person-centered care that prioritizes the preferences and needs of each person? If so, how do they achieve this?
- What is the level of regular planned activity? (Ask to see an activities calendar and facility newsletter.)
- Is there a spiritual emphasis at the facility—chaplains, worship services, and faith-based programming?[6]

Encourage caregivers to begin the process of reviewing options long before they feel a decision must be made. This avoids having to make a quick decision during a time of crisis, giving them time to reach a high degree of comfort with the decision. You can also suggest that they reach out to other caregivers during this evaluation and transition process. A formal or informal support group of caregivers in your church could help provide support, education, and camaraderie during this challenging discernment time. Hearing the stories of others who are successfully walking the caregiving path is a great resource for caregivers.

Ministers and church leaders play an important role in helping caregivers—listening, counseling, supporting, and connecting. Take time to learn about senior adult care facilities in your community so that when caregivers are ready to discuss options, you can provide reliable information. Continuing care retirement communities—communities that offer independent living, assisted living, and skilled nursing care—usually offer memory support units, areas dedicated to the care of people living with dementia diseases. There are also independent assisted living facilities with memory support units. Some people may need skilled nursing care settings.

Most importantly, be nonjudgmental at this time. Each caregiver needs to decide what is best for him or her. She may not handle things the way you would if you were the caregiver, and that's fine. Perhaps she's ready to begin going back out with friends or traveling. Perhaps she's ready not to be the sole caregiver shouldering responsibility. Alternatively, she may feel she's the only one who should do it and push herself to continue. We need to be supportive of these personal decisions—while still watching, though, for health concerns that necessitate considering alternatives before a crisis occurs.

Help with relocating a loved one, when or if needed.

If the time comes for a caregiver to move his loved one to a facility that offers memory support, be there to provide emotional and spiritual support, but also assistance with the logistics of the actual physical move. Have people in place to help as needed. This is another area where research can be helpful. In our community there are several companies that focus solely on helping seniors move. Their specialized sensibility and experience removes a great deal of stress. There is probably such a business in your area as well. Look into it and be prepared with this information ahead of time to offer to caregivers as they begin to think about a potential move for their loved one.

Know your boundaries.

Finally, you cannot be all things for all people. When ministering to caregivers of people with dementia, know what you can and can't do. This is why a team approach is so valuable, as different members can meet different needs and provide care in various areas. This is also where research will come in handy, as you familiarize yourself with resources to which you can refer others. Strive for balance in this area, trusting that God will use you to minister to caregivers in the ways they need most.

Chapter 9

A CHURCH-WIDE RESPONSE

*T*hroughout this book, you've encountered many approaches and ideas that will help you, as an individual, minister to families facing serious memory challenges. Let's look now at ways that faith communities can work together to respond.

Each day, 10,000 people reach the age of sixty-five.[1] For many churches, this means that a large percentage of your members are now, or soon will be, over this threshold. Economists and health care providers alike tell us that many of these people will live longer than ever before. This is a double-edged sword: On one hand, with increasing life expectancy comes the exciting prospect of rethinking what aging means. Indeed, "vibrancy" is the new "aging." Yet on the other hand, as expressed in previous chapters, age-wave predictions also include sobering facts about the increased likelihood of dementia, which will affect 50 percent of people eighty-five years of age and older. It is expected that by 2050, nearly 14 million Americans will suffer from some form of serious memory loss, a three-fold increase from 2016.[2]

Whole families are affected by dementia diseases, not just the person with the diagnosis. As the rate of dementia diagnoses increases, caregiving demands will rise along with accompanying emotional, physical, social, spiritual, and financial tolls. While these realities can remain invisible, hidden away behind the closed doors of individual households, communities of faith can learn to intentionally recognize need and discern a call to minister to families in life-giving ways. Literally millions of people stand in need of outreach and churches that will answer God's call to serve one another in love and faithfulness.

Unfortunately, few churches have recognized this deep and growing need. Yet the opportunities for spiritual growth are rich. As a church reaches out to people with dementia and their caregivers, opportunities abound for community interaction, intergenerational experience, and practical service. And yes, even for church growth!

To meet this tsunami of needs, it's going to take an intentional church-wide response. It's going to mean creating a climate where all are welcome, even if they might need to get up and pace or ask the same question repeatedly. Creating an open, safe, and accepting church environment where people can remain active members of their faith community for as long as possible is a worthy effort as we seek to reflect God's abiding love. How wonderful it would be to nurture a dementia-friendly church where members experiencing these diseases could stay engaged and included and not feel isolated and excluded.

HOW CAN CHURCHES RESPOND
TO THIS GROWING NEED?

Know your church members.

Keep track and keep in touch. Taking note of church attendance is a critically important basic step in developing a ministry of connection to families coping with dementia issues. Does your church track family relationships? Do you note when family systems change, thus changing patterns in attendance? Community response relies on recognizing patterns and needs, even while respecting privacy and confidentiality. How can your church best convey true concern and track involvement in order to respond in love?

Create a safe and friendly environment.

Consider inviting someone from the Alzheimer's Association to assess your church's facilities for safety and accessibility for people living with dementia. Challenges in physical ability, judgment and sensory perception can lead to injury if the environment isn't carefully monitored for things which could prove to be dangerous. Rather than expecting someone with dementia to adapt to challenging surroundings, we can make necessary adaptations to anticipate their needs. Some things for consideration: Are ramps needed? Are there adequate railings on the steps? Is lighting sufficient? If you have a parishioner with dementia who wanders, does the church have alarms on its doors? Are bathrooms handicapped accessible and free of hazardous materials?

Collect and lend resources.

One of the simplest but most powerful ways a faith community can respond is by providing a list of resources and a collection of materials people can access. This book provides a bibliography of suggested reading. Consider collecting or purchasing titles to add to your church library or keep with a pastor or ministry group. Similarly, a small group of volunteers can meet twice a year to compile and update a list of organizations in your region whose services are dedicated to seniors. The list might include some of the following:

- Doctors and clinics specializing in gerontology
- Senior living organizations such as continuing care retirement communities, assisted living, memory support centers and skilled nursing facilities. Each of these will be happy to provide materials for your collection and an annual outreach can update contact information.
- Your local Area Agency on Aging, Alzheimer's Association, senior day care centers, Meals on Wheels, Habitat for Humanity, Medicare programs, and state LeadingAge chapter.

Information is power, and often when people are overwhelmed and frightened they do not access information adequately. Systematically and intentionally gathering resources to share—and making people aware of your resource bank—is a tremendous service.

Another way to provide needed resources is to create a medical equipment recycling room at your church. As a family is ready to discard equipment no longer needed—shower chairs, electric lift chairs, grabbers, portable commodes—store them for the next person in need. Then, deliver the needed items with a healthy meal.

These are just a few ideas. The possibilities are many as we observe and listen. The more time you spend with those in your community who are living with dementia diseases, the more opportunities you will find to provide resources and meet needs that have been overlooked.

Offer instruction and support to members and your community.

When Words Fail offers an instructional demonstration video and study guide for educating clergy, lay leaders, and caregivers (available at www.whenwordsfail.com). This is best offered in group settings so that discussion can occur. Other educational materials are suggested in the back of this book. Decide how often to offer opportunities for learning about these topics through coordination with your faith community's educational ministry. Perhaps you could offer a seminar at your church led by someone from your local Alzheimer's Association. Consider inviting neighboring churches to join you.

Ongoing opportunities for education about dementia and spiritual care are needed. As the members of your faith community receive information concerning dementia diseases and their effects, they will gain understanding and insight on how to relate to people better. Simply offering regularly scheduled educational opportunities will send a powerful signal to your faith community that your church is concerned and striving to understand the challenges of life with dementia.

Get involved in finding a cure.

Each year the Alzheimer's Association holds community-wide walks to end Alzheimer's disease. Mobilizing church members to walk together can send a powerful message of love and support to caregivers and their loved ones. Find details about when the Walk to End Alzheimer's is scheduled for your area by visiting www.alz.org/walk.

Learn about and then encourage congregation members living with dementia and their caregivers to consider taking part in clinical trials for dementia research. A clinical trial is a step-by-step process that studies or tests a new procedure, drug, vaccine, or device for prevention, treatment, screening, and improving quality of life. Such trials move research forward to find effective treatments and cures for diseases. Increasing participation in clinical trials for dementia research is vitally important, especially among minority populations. According to UsAgainstAlzheimer's statistics, compared to white Americans, African Americans are twice as likely, and Latinos 1.5 times as likely, to develop Alzheimer's disease. The Centers for Disease Control and Prevention reveals that between 1999 and 2014, Alzheimer's deaths increased by 55 percent among all Americans, but they increased 99 percent for African American and 107 percent for Latinos. Encouraging church members to consider trials may make a true difference.[3]

Take stock of your church's existing resources.

What is going on within your church that could be used to serve families coping with dementia? Chances are there are many existing resources that could be redirected to help meet the needs of caregivers and their loved ones.

Perhaps your church hosts a scout troop interested in service projects. Why not encourage them to paint a caregiver's fence, bring over groceries, or, if appropriate, visit with a dementia patient?

Do you keep an active list of members willing to provide occasional meals for members-in-need? Make sure that caregivers and members with dementia are on the list and adequately provided for.

Do you have an active adult Sunday school or discipleship group that could be empowered to provide care? Put them in touch with caregivers to discuss how they might work together.

Do you have prayer groups that could be enlisted to pray for people living with dementia and their caregivers, both within the church and the greater community? Provide them with a list of prayer requests that can be updated as needed.

Are there service groups and service days dedicated to practical projects? Perhaps your faith community gathers to assemble school bags for children in need or kits for people facing medical treatments. Consider arranging for your memory-challenged members to participate.

Are there singing groups willing to perform as a full group or in small sections? Help facilitate a musical performance for members with dementia and their caregivers.

What about your nurseries, preschools, and Sunday school programs? Consider enlisting the children's ministry to write encouraging cards or draw pictures for members with dementia. Facilitate opportunities for young adults to be involved in ministry as well, perhaps by helping deliver meals or organizing participation in the annual Alzheimer's walk.

Do you have a church bus or a list of people willing to drive members to church? Connect them to caregivers and establish regular routines to help those with dementia make it to services and other events.

The opportunities to use already-existing ministries are endless and unique to each church. Keep looking and dreaming, and encourage others in the community to consider ways in which they might use established programs and ministries to directly serve those with dementia and memory loss.

Congregational respite care

Looking for a way to support caregivers of people living with dementia? Your church could consider offering a respite care program. Respite means a short period of rest or relief. For your church, respite could mean providing several hours of care one day a month, once a week, or several days a week for loved ones and caregivers of people experiencing dementia. As your church provides a safe and secure environment, participants can enjoy stimulation and fellowship with new people in a place filled with God's love. For caregivers who are caring every day, both day and night, respite could mean time for rest and relaxation or taking care of business, errand running, or fellowship with friends and family

First United Methodist Church in Montgomery, Alabama is one example of a church which is successfully providing respite care. Six years ago, after enlisting and then training volunteers in dementia care, this church began a two-day-a-week, four-hour-a-day respite ministry under the direction of church member Daphne Johnston. Since then, their respite program has grown to a four-day-a-week program involving volunteers from eight local churches and two synagogues. Each day twelve to fifteen volunteers participate with an average of twenty-five attendees as they enjoy art, music, movement, intergenerational experiences, pet therapy, prayer, devotions, choir, service projects, exercise, and a host of other activities, including lunch. Most importantly, participants thrive from being together and building relationships with each other and volunteers.

More than one hundred caregivers attend a monthly support group at First United Methodist, held while their loved ones are in respite care. Volunteers in this program average 1,100 hours of service a year.[4] Your church can start modestly and build your respite program as needs present and volunteers are able.

Encourage and assist families in completing legal and financial planning.

As mentioned briefly in chapter four, establishing a medical and durable power of attorney and advance directive is extremely important for people with dementia diseases and their families. Your church might want to offer a seminar for the church and local community on legal and financial planning. Invite trained professionals to help. Most likely, people with this expertise are within your church's membership or can be easily found by a member.

When someone starts exhibiting memory loss, the need for families to do this kind of planning is acute. While the person can still make decisions for herself, it's good to get in writing what her desires are for her future care and who she wants to make decisions for her when she no longer can. It is always better for people to be able to self-determine rather than have other peoples' wills and desires imposed upon them during a time of crisis. When difficult decisions need to be made later, having the person's wishes in writing provides caregivers with the information they need to make decisions that honor their loved one. By providing information about financial planning ahead of time through seminars and other educational opportunities, you can help families avoid potential conflict or stress later, when the loved one is no longer able to express his wishes.

Provide support groups at your church, or go with caregivers to outside support groups.

Offer your church's facilities to the local chapter of the Alzheimer's Association for a new support group location. This could be a needed resource for both your church family and your broader community. Some locations offer a support group for caregivers, while a group for their loved ones takes place simultaneously in a different room. Volunteers who have received training in dementia care could provide a music time, devotional, snacks, and other activities for people living with dementia diseases.

Keep in mind that some caregivers, especially men, are hesitant to attend support groups. Although they might recognize they could benefit from encouragement and support from people going through similar circumstances, the thought of going into a room full of strangers and feeling vulnerable may be too daunting. In such cases, you might volunteer to go with the caregiver to a support group. He might be more likely to go, knowing a friend and support is there with him. Over time, as he sees how valuable the sharing, input, and encouragement is, he'll feel confident to go on his own.

Throughout my work with families facing dementia, I've realized that an important form of support for spouses, in particular, is encouragement to continue enjoying and participating in what gives them joy as individuals. This balance is often difficult for spouses to find and may be made harder when they are not supported in their need to spend time with friends or enjoy activities that are affirming to them.

At Westminster Canterbury Richmond, a group of men meets regularly to support one another through the delicate and difficult balance of loving their wives through their journey with dementia and taking time for themselves. This group started with only a few men, but over several years it has grown to almost twenty members. As mentioned in the previous chapter, as spiritual care providers, we may tend to focus most of our efforts on the person living with dementia at the expense of the spouse or other loved ones. This wonderful group of men reminds me to bear in mind the real needs of family members whose lives are deeply and permanently affected and who must be valued and affirmed as individuals whose lives we celebrate. Is there an opportunity to create a support group like this one within your church community?

Offer the joy of music, through a choir created for a special purpose.

Music offers an exciting and fulfilling arena for a church-wide response. Around the country, a number of organizations and churches have developed choirs for people with dementia and their caregivers. Dr. Mark Patterson, director of music at Salisbury Presbyterian Church in Midlothian, Virginia, noticed that even as several members of various adult choirs at the church began to experience dementia, they continued to thrive in the choir with small but thoughtful amounts of intervention.[5] One particular parishioner's experience astounded Patterson. "One of our Chancel Choir members with rather advanced dementia has been able to sing the Mozart Requiem in Latin and sing all of our repertoire. She still comes to chancel choir rehearsals regularly, even though she has had to drop out of most other activities in her life." Not only did

Patterson find this amazing, it inspired him to pursue additional ways to reach out to others with dementia.

A presentation by Giving Voice Chorus at the American Choral Directors Association conference sparked Patterson's interest. Giving Voice Chorus is a program founded by Mary Lenard and Marge Ostroushko and developed in collaboration with the MacPhail Center for Music in Minneapolis and St. Paul, Minnesota. Lenard and Ostroushko both cared for parents with dementia and recognized the positive effects of music in their caretaking journey. The Giving Voice Chorus established its first chorus in 2014 and a second in 2016 for people with dementia and their caregivers and, through the Giving Voice Initiative, provides a toolkit for organizations who wish to start a chorus.[6] Patterson felt called to explore this further, as a natural extension of what his church was providing for a few people. He and his team have named this church's new choir, which will be open to members from throughout the region, the Joyful Voices choir.

Other churches experience success with such a choir. First United Methodist Church in Montgomery, Alabama, mentioned earlier in this chapter, offers the Side by Side choir for caregivers and loved ones with dementia. Sixty singers participate in this dynamic group.

Emerging research underscores the validity of music programs for people with dementia. The medial frontal cortex of the brain seems to link music, memories, and emotions. This cortex is one of the last brain regions to deteriorate in Alzheimer's disease patients. This may be why people with the disease can often remember, enjoy, and respond to music when other memories are lost.[7] We provide information about new research on this subject in the final section of this book.

New York University's Center for Cognitive Neurology Professor Dr. Mary Mittelman is exploring theories that music actually activates parts of the brain that dementia does not touch until the later stages. She founded a choir named The Unforgettables to study the effects of music on dementia patients. Further research is underway, but there can be no doubt that music groups such as The Unforgettables demonstrate the joyful effect of music and in coming together to sing.[8]

At the new Johns Hopkins Center for Music and Medicine, professors and students from the medical school and Peabody Institute are collaborating in multidisciplinary work that emphasizes innovation and community connection. Their early findings with the ParkinSonics, a choir formed for people with Parkinson's Disease, demonstrate positive results. The Center is studying the effects that singing has on dementia patients and their caregivers, using a one-on-one model the Center calls "side-by-side singing." Their goal is to add more knowledge to a growing body of work on how music can heal.[9]

The leaders of these choirs emphasize the importance of including a caregiver with every singer. This pairing allows for a shared positive experience and for adequate encouragement and assistance. Joanne Sherman, who directs Salisbury Presbyterian Church's Joyful Voices, cites another reason for the one-on-one pairing. "We incorporate rhythm, movement, and breathing exercises to enhance the experience and make a positive impact on physical health. And this is much easier with a partner."[10]

Receiving a dementia diagnosis is a frightening experience, and typically both the person affected and their loved ones are filled with dread about experiences that must eventually be abandoned. "Participating in Joyful Voices is something they *can* do, and something that the person with Alzheimer's or dementia and their caregiver can enjoy doing together," says Mark Patterson. Perhaps your church can explore ways to allow music to remain a joyful part of life for your members with dementia.

Allow members with dementia as much participation as possible within your faith community.

Howard has been a deacon in his Baptist church for many of his seventy-eight years. Now that he's living with Alzheimer's disease, he has trouble remembering things, and this Sunday, he forgot how to pass the offering plates up and down the pew rows. What used to be so familiar to him now causes confusion, and a look of panic settles on his face. Noticing this, his best friend, George, slips to his side and gently assists him. Once they reach the back of the church and the last pew, George helps

Howard join the other deacons who are gathered to walk back down the
aisle. They subtly help him, too, once they're at the front of the church,
and thank him for his assistance. Howard returns to his pew with a look
of contentment on his face.

For as long as possible, it is important to let people who are experiencing dementia continue to engage in ministry roles that have been crucial ways they serve people and God. Sometimes you may need to gracefully transfer them into another church role that you know they'll enjoy, while someone else "tries out" their old role for a specified time period. Often once they're in their new, less stressful role, they'll be relieved and not mind the switch. It requires creativity, diplomacy, and compassion. As you educate your faith community about dementia, they will become more able to respond compassionately to challenging situations. Everyone will benefit from continuing to nurture one another, regardless of what physical roadblock seems to be in the way.

Invite affected families to participate in the life of the congregation.

Make a special effort to invite families coping with dementia to participate in congregational events. Church programs, concerts, plays, preschool programs, even the rehearsals for these events can be wonderful opportunities to help them feel included. Don't assume they will realize they are welcome—make a special effort to invite them through phone calls and notes. Perhaps you can help arrange transportation. Have extra volunteers ready and prepared to assist people as needed. If attending events is truly difficult or impossible for people, consider recording them and delivering a DVD to the caregiver so he can enjoy it with his loved one in their home. Regularly delivering a recording of services can be life-giving to those who cannot attend church services, should the caregiver not have access to the Internet. Even if caregivers can download content themselves, the value of a personal visit can never be underestimated.

Decide how to serve, and then organize the effort.

If your church is interested in forming a ministry dedicated to serving people experiencing dementia and their caregivers, start by forming a small group to examine options and resources and prayerfully consider ministry opportunities. Create a plan and methodically work toward coordination. Collaborate with other church communities and regional nonprofit organizations. It is often rare for faith communities to actively and intentionally serve in this manner that your church will make a true and needed difference. You *will* inspire others. But be realistic. Start small, see what works, and grow as you are able. Pray regularly for God's guidance and blessing. Trust God's Spirit to strengthen, sustain, and guide your efforts.

Pray.

Never underestimate the power of ongoing prayer. Encourage your pastors, lay leaders and congregants to remember in prayer those who travel the path of memory loss. Pray about those living with dementia and their families from the pulpit, during Sunday school, at prayer meetings, and individually. Pray for your church's response.

Act.

You've learned, evaluated, and considered. You've reached out and taken stock. You've prayed and felt a call to serve. You've recruited and organized. Now *act*. Step out in faith! Knowing that needs are deep, decide what your church can and will do. Likely you can do a few things well, but not everything. In Jesus's name, move forward! And keep track of your efforts, as this is a great encouragement for sustainability.

Share ideas with one another.

We can help one another through sharing successes and challenges. As more churches begin to address the needs of those with dementia, we can learn from and encourage each other in the process. Please join us and share your community's efforts at our website: www.whenwordsfail.com. "Therefore encourage one another and build each other up, just as in fact you are doing" (1 Thessalonians 5:11, NIV).

Chapter 10

CASE STUDIES

ometimes, looking at scenarios and thinking ahead about how we might respond can help us respond well in similar, real-life situations. Remember, though, that everyone is different and responds differently. We can never truly predict how anyone will respond based on how they are feeling physically, emotionally, and spiritually on any given day. With God's help, and a heart full of love, we're called to do the best we can to meet someone's needs and show compassion.

Consider the following case studies as discussion starters. Based on what you've learned in the previous chapters, how might you respond? (Following the case studies you'll find suggested solutions for consideration and discussion.)

CASE STUDY #1

Ninety-five-year-old Sloan Hastings has dementia and chronic obstructive pulmonary disorder (COPD). She lives with her daughter Amber, and has been a member of your church for decades. Sloan has been sitting in her bedroom for two days now, with the curtains drawn and lights off. A spry and energetic woman, Sloan is usually active, chatty, and upbeat. You haven't seen her in a few weeks, and today when you visit, she immediately asks you to sit down and reaches for your hand.

"Why can't I just die? Why doesn't God just take me?" she laments. "Let me see the psychiatrist. He'll know what to give me to make it stop. I'm losing my mind, you know. I'm not good for anything anymore."

Sloan seems to be in despair. Before you went into her room, her daughter told you that over the last six months Sloan has been experiencing significant short-term memory loss. Earlier in the week, the doctor diagnosed her as having dementia. Now, after squeezing your hand for a while and staring at her husband's picture on the wall, she finally starts reminiscing about what she used to do, when her mind was sharp. Gradually her eyes light up and her voice lilts with excitement as she shares, "I was a social worker in the city, helping kids. I used to do sit-ins, too, you know. I was active in NOW, the National Organization for Women. We helped make sure women could get good jobs. I was so busy."

"I miss my home, too," she reflects. "We lived down on the James River. I was always outside with my flowers, animals, and the glorious water."

She begins to cry. "Now what do I do?" she asks. "Just sit here wasting space and money? I can't even remember what I had for breakfast. Did I eat breakfast?

"What good am I? I can't help anybody. I don't even know what I had for breakfast." She looks at you. "Will you help me?" she pleads.

Questions to consider:

1. What stage of dementia is Sloan experiencing—early, middle, late?

2. What are her emotional needs? Spiritual needs?

3. How could you address her emotional and spiritual needs?

CASE STUDY #2

Betty, an eighty-two-year-old woman with vascular dementia, lives in an almost constant state of anxiety. Her confusion and agitated behavior peak every day at 3:00 pm. At that time each day she paces, wrings her hands, and stands by the locked doors of her memory-support household.

Even at other times, Betty's brow is furrowed with worry, and she rarely shows positive emotions. She can express herself verbally but not always understandably. Her children rarely come to visit anymore because it's hard for them to see her this way. She used to be their happy, sweet, and fun-loving mom.

Betty grew up attending the Methodist church in her hometown, where she taught Sunday school and ran the food pantry. She loves singing old hymns and responds to sitting outside in the sunshine. Dark, rainy days seem to exacerbate her confusion and agitation.

Staff try to distract Betty when she's most anxious, and it sometimes works.

Questions to consider:

1. What stage of dementia is Betty experiencing—early, middle, late?

2. What are her emotional needs? Spiritual needs?

3. How could you address her emotional and spiritual needs?

CASE STUDY #3

Whitt Moore, an eighty-eight-year-old Anglican gentleman originally from England, is in bed now, unable to do anything for himself. His eyes are closed and his eyebrows occasionally furrow. Whitt's breathing is irregular, and he occasionally thrashes restlessly and moans. For the last week, he has not eaten or drunk anything. The nurses in the nursing care center where he lives don't know how he's holding on to life.

Whitt's only son visits as often as he can, which is not too often since he lives out of state. So, he is mostly alone. From visits over the past several years, when he was more lucid, you know that Whitt grew up in London and loved the Book of Common Prayer. He told you at an earlier time that he loved living in the city where he could attend lots of cultural events, from the symphony to the opera and ballet. Whitt also enjoyed breeding and raising Jack Russell terriers. They often roamed London's parks together.

Questions to consider:
1. What stage of dementia is Mr. Moore experiencing—early, middle or late?

2. What are his emotional needs? Spiritual?

3. How could you address his emotional and spiritual needs?

CASE STUDY #4

Karen is exhausted. Living five miles from her parents used to be fine. It was great when the kids were little and they'd help out with childcare. But now everything is going wrong. Karen's husband, Dave, travels with his job. Her parents, the Browns, have aged and have significant health issues. At eighty, Mr. Brown has had three heart attacks over the last five years. He's frequently out of breath and will soon need oxygen. Macular degeneration makes it impossible for him to do his favorite pastime, reading, or help with many household chores. Mrs. Brown has Alzheimer's disease. She's forgotten how to cook and speaking is getting more and more difficult each day. She's up and down all night, wandering the halls or playing the piano like she's at church playing for the choir. Mr. Brown admits he doesn't know what to do.

Karen shops, cooks many meals for them, handles the yard work, drives them to appointments, does their laundry, and many other chores. She accomplishes all of this while juggling a part-time job at the local library. Lately she's been spending the night several nights a week to let her dad sleep when her mom is up, restless, in the middle of the night. Karen hardly has time to see her new grand-son who lives in the next town.

Karen's own physical health is starting to be compromised as she goes nonstop—not to mention her emotional well-being. Going to church and participating in service projects used to give her joy, but more and more she misses worship and activities. No one from church seems to even notice she's gone. Her parent's church, where they've been lifelong members, has tried reaching out to the Browns. Mr. Brown always responds, "We're fine. Karen is such a wonderful daughter. She's helping us."

Karen's relationship with her husband is suffering because resent-ment is building up. He seems oblivious to her parents' increasing needs and is unappreciative of all that Karen does to care for them. Adding to the strain, Karen's mother constantly criticizes Karen for not doing things "right."

Karen secretly dreams of "wringing the neck" of her sister, who lives across town but sees their parents sporadically. Her sister's idea of helping is to grab a bucket of chicken from a fast-food chain and come visit their folks on an occasional Sunday afternoon. She throws the paper plates in the trash, but that's the extent of her "help."

Questions to consider:

1. What kind of physical, emotional, and spiritual needs do you think Karen has? Her parents?

2. How might you help address those needs?

3. How might your church address those needs?

CASE STUDY #5

Annie, an eighty-eight-year-old woman, lives alone. Her husband, Joe, died ten years ago. Until he died, the Cape Cod-style cottage they'd lived in for fifty years was immaculate. Together they maintained the best yard on the block. Roses and hydrangeas bloomed everywhere. They were always proud to show people around and held an annual neighborhood picnic in their backyard. Since they never had children, and their siblings had died, they treated neighbors and friends like family. Children were always welcome and cookies were always available after school.

In recent years, Annie has not been doing so well. Two years ago she received a dementia diagnosis while in the hospital following a fall. She's stooped and arthritic. Walking is slow and painful. Once friendly and engaging, Annie barely speaks to folks in the small town's grocery store. She used to spend hours conversing with everyone. Sometimes she's even curt if a child bumps into her cart or the shelf is not stocked just right. People notice her layers of clothes, even in the warmest weather, and her car seems to be falling apart with each block she drives.

She doesn't come out of the house much anymore. Unread newspapers are piled in the driveway and weeds choke the flower beds. When neighbors stop by, bringing food or wanting to check on Annie, they're often turned away and never invited in. Neighbors say she doesn't recognize them when they visit and seems to look at them with fear and suspicion. People are becoming more and more concerned about her safety and well-being, but they don't know what to do to help.

Although the couple had no personal church affiliation, they live near the town's Presbyterian church, which they attended on special holidays with their nearest neighbor.

Questions to consider:

1. What stage of dementia is Annie experiencing—early, middle or late?

2. What kind of physical, emotional, and spiritual needs might Annie have?

3. Could a neighborhood church respond to Annie's needs? If so, what might they do?

CASE STUDY SOLUTIONS

Case Study #1

Sloan is in the early stages of dementia. She's experiencing short-term memory loss and confusion. On this day, she's feeling despair and lack of self-worth. She's discouraged and frustrated by her lack of ability to do things she feels would add value to society. She's sad because of what she has lost—her home on the river, animals, lifestyle, her role as an advocate for people, her ability to get up and go. Spiritually, she's feeling abandoned ("Why doesn't God just take me?"), unworthy, and unlovable. But Sloan also expresses joy, pride, and accomplishment when she talks about her past role as an advocate for children and women.

First, after listening, acknowledge her feelings and tell her how honored you are that she could share them with you. Assure her of your, and your congregation's, concern and care. Tell her how sorry you are that she's feeling down and discouraged. Invite her to share more with you. She obviously wants to talk about past contributions to society. See if she'll talk more about them.

Thank her for all that she did to help others and affirm what that must have meant to them. Ask if she's comfortable with you sharing some of her accomplishments with others. Explain that this might encourage others or inspire them to help. (If she says yes, share about her accomplishments—not about her discouragement and sadness—with caregivers and friends who might visit to hear her stories, too.) Continue listening, and offering gentle touch as you hold hands. Ask if she'd like for you to pray with her. When you need to leave, assure her of God's presence and love and ask to come back again.

On another visit, you might ask to record her talking about the social work she did. Find out from Sloan what brings her comfort, hope, and peace. If it's Scripture reading, read some uplifting passages, encouraging her to talk about how they make her feel. Perhaps devotional literature appeals to her; if so, you could read some together. Do things with her that nurture her spirit.

Sometimes people just need a compassionate listener—someone who won't judge them for feeling down and discouraged. It's OK not to have all the answers. However, since Sloan is questioning God and her worthiness to live, talk with your minister following this visit. Know when to make a referral. Whenever people say anything about wanting to end their life, you must tell someone in authority. The minister can follow up, helping explore those issues further.

Case Study #2

Betty is in the middle stages of dementia. Anxiety, confusion, and worry seem to be the main emotions she experiences. Spiritually, she's in need of reassurance and comfort. To help her feel less anxious, she needs to know that she is secure and loved. Although she may not be able to articulate it, she misses her children and friends who rarely visit. Feeling abandoned and lonely could heighten her confusion and anxiety.

As you reach out to her children to offer support and encouragement to them, you might explore with them what happened in Betty's earlier life each day at 3:00 pm. Their reflections might be able to explain why Betty's so especially anxious that time each day. Can you imagine something that might happen at that time each day? You may have guessed it: school letting out. Betty has three children. Her youngest, Jeff, has mental and physical disabilities. Each day at 3:00 pm he arrived home from school on the bus. Someone needed to be there to greet him and resume his care. So, at this stage in Betty's dementia, she's convinced that's where she needs to be. Because of her language difficulty, she can't articulate that.

In talking with her family you learn these things and find out that a neighbor, Tina, often helped with Jeff. When Betty had an appointment and couldn't meet his bus, Tina met it and brought Jeff home until Betty arrived. She was a trusted and loving friend. You share this information with the staff, and now, most days when Betty is anxious at 3:00 pm and wringing her hands, staff reassure her that Tina is meeting Jeff today. Automatically she physically relaxes and lets them help her to a chair where she sits and listens to some traditional hymns, or she goes outside to relax.

When you visit, you might try to avoid that highly anxious time of day for Betty. If you do go around 3:00, you know what's going on and how to help. On your visits you can plan to listen to and sing music with her, take walks outside in the garden, read scripture, and pray with her (which her family told you were important aspects of Betty's faith).

Over time, Betty begins to respond with joy when she sees you and to enjoy your times together. If she gets very anxious or agitated, you do the things that usually bring her comfort. If they fail one day, though, you could ask the nurse for assistance, or tell Betty you love her and will return another day. Be sure to come back if you say you're going to.

Case Study #3

Whitt is in the late stages of dementia, near the end of his earthly life. He can no longer take care of his basic needs. Because communication with words is no longer possible for Whitt, he is not able to say how he feels. It will therefore be important to carefully observe his body language. For example, furrowing eyebrows can indicate pain and discomfort, as can thrashing and moaning. You may want to mention these observations to his caregivers in case they have medications that might help or want to notify the doctor. He cannot tell you his emotional needs, but thrashing in the bed could indicate anxiety or frustration. Because his son can't be with him, he may feel lonely or sad.

Because you know he is a devout Anglican and he has asked you, in the past, to read favorite scriptures and prayers from the Book of Common Prayer, you know these things provide him with comfort and peace. You know that he enjoys music, and it nurtures his spirit. Keeping all of this in mind, read the prayers of the sick or prayers of the dying to Whitt from the Book of Common Prayer. Read Psalm 23 and other comforting psalms. Since you've learned he loves music, play some soft religious, classical, or operatic music for him.

Talk with him in a low, comforting voice about how much you enjoy visiting him, how you feel God's presence with him. Pray God's loving arms will enfold him in an eternal embrace. If you know he likes touch, place your hand gently on his arm for reassurance. Don't feel like you have to say much, though; he will feel your loving presence with him, and that will bring comfort. This is a very holy time. It is enough to just sit quietly beside his bed, saying nothing, and praying silently for his eternal rest and peace with the God he loves and who loves him.

Case Study #4

Karen is not just physically exhausted, due to lack of sleep from being up with her mom many nights; she's emotionally exhausted, too. She's feeling frustrated, angry, and overwhelmed while doing everything single-handedly for her parents, since neither her husband nor sister are helping. Coupled with her family's inattentiveness, Karen feels her church has forgotten and abandoned her. Church friends seem unconcerned about where she is, much less what's keeping her away.

Spiritually, Karen needs love and tender care from both her family and church. She needs physical, emotional, and spiritual support so she doesn't feel so alone. She needs someone she can trust to help support her. Karen needs someone to listen to her and walk alongside her. Her church family's support could remind her of God's love for her and presence with her during this difficult time.

Mr. Brown has multiple health problems—heart trouble, shortness of breath, and macular degeneration—which heighten his dependence on Karen. The effects of Mrs. Brown's increasing dementia have left him feeling overwhelmed and emotionally paralyzed about how to respond. He is unrealistic about what Karen can do, as he relies on her for everything. We don't know exactly why he's turned away offers of help from church members, but Mr. Brown needs to trust his church family enough to let them help support the family.

Alzheimer's disease has compromised Mrs. Brown's abilities to perform normal activities of daily living, thus making it hard for her to care for the household and her husband. Her frustrations about memory loss and losing control are causing her to lash out angrily and critically at Karen, the one person who's trying desperately to help. Mrs. Brown needs to be assured of

God's loving presence with her through expressions of support from people besides Karen. Notice that she has no other physical issues. Because the average duration of Alzheimer's disease is eight years, with the potential of up to twenty, their church would do well to form a support team who will be able to journey with the family.

The Brown's church has offered to help, but they've fallen short of looking beyond her dad's assurances that they're "fine." By talking with Karen, whom they've also known for years, church friends can get a list of ways they might help: laundry, yard work, grocery shopping, meal preparation, respite care so Karen can have a break, providing rides to doctor appointments, reading to Mr. Brown, or playing music with Mrs. Brown.

Upon talking with Karen, you learn that she is beginning to contemplate the need for her parents to either move in with her and Dave or move into an assisted living facility. She doesn't know where to begin. The church could provide her with resources it has collected from various sources, and you could advise her to contact the Alzheimer's Association to talk about her situation. Referrals can be made for community services—Meals on Wheels, senior home help, and other in-home services—that could make their, and Karen's, life much easier.

The two churches could be involved here: Karen's church could reach out to her, offering emotional and spiritual support and encouragement. Perhaps Karen's minister could help facilitate a family meeting where Karen could voice concerns and ask for much-needed help. The family could also discuss legal and medical decisions that need to be made. Her parent's church could offer more tangible support to Mr. and Mrs. Brown, along with emotional and spiritual support. One role you might be able to play in cases such as this is facilitating communication and action between the two churches.

Case Study #5

Annie is in the middle stages of dementia. She is in physical pain from her rheumatoid arthritis, and perhaps from aftereffects from the fall she experienced two years ago. She's emotionally suffering from isolation, withdrawal, anxiety, confusion, memory loss, anger, and fear.

Annie isn't a regular church attender, and we don't know much about her personal faith. She may not be able to tell you now. We do know that she loves God's creation and carefully tended to it for as long as she could. We know that Annie was generous and did many acts of kindness for adults and children. She got to know people and nurture them. Annie and her husband, Joe, knew how to care for others. Because she can no longer do any of those things that she loved, we can only assume she's suffering spiritual distress and perhaps feeling some helplessness and despair.

Annie needs help, but in her confusion and anxiety she can't reach out or accept it. As Christians we are to be ambassadors of God's love to all people. Annie's neighbors are reaching out to her, but the church has not yet come alongside them to help facilitate and expand this support network.

Sadly, this kind of situation is not unusual. If we look around our communities we can see older people having trouble making ends meet, isolating themselves, having physical difficulty getting around, and displaying signs of dementia diseases. If we look around our churches we see older adults living alone, too, with little or no support. What happens to them when they are facing these situations alone? They need neighbors and friends who are watching out for them like you and me.

Knowing that we can't meet all of their needs, what do we do? In Annie's case, perhaps the church she sometimes visited, or another neighbor's church, could coordinate efforts to assist her. The minister or lay church leader could contact the local Alzheimer's chapter or Area Agency on Aging for advice and direction. Maybe someone at one of those organizations could attempt to contact Annie to begin some care coordination.

Church members and neighbors could volunteer to clean up her once-beautiful yard, perform needed car and home repairs, purchase and deliver groceries, or cook meals for her. Granted, she may not accept the help, but if people keep calmly and persistently showing their concern—perhaps showing up with a lawn mower one day to do the work—Annie might grow more comfortable with accepting assistance. Hopefully she'll begin to see and feel how much people love and care for her.

Unfortunately, it sometimes takes another accident or illness that puts a person in the hospital to ultimately get them the help they need. Once there, hospital care coordinators will discern if it's safe for the person to go home alone. The hospital is mandated to get her the care she needs to live safely and as best she can, so that might be what it takes for someone like Annie to receive adequate care.

Whether she is in the hospital or at home, people should continue to reach out to her with love and compassion. She will hopefully be able to see God's love shining through us.

Chapter 11

SAMPLE WORSHIP SERVICES
AND DEVOTIONS

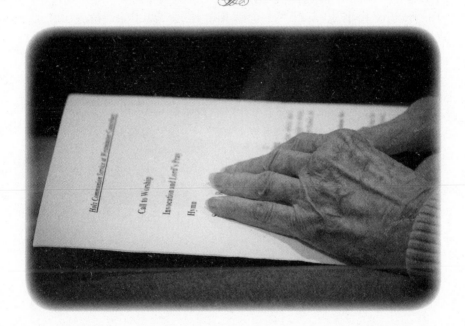

As I've mentioned several times throughout this book, there may be an occasion when your church has the opportunity to conduct a worship service or devotion time with people experiencing dementia in a local skilled nursing care, assisted living, or long-term care facility. If several of your church members live in one such facility, this is a wonderful opportunity to volunteer to provide a service. Other church members could come to sit amongst residents and participate, offer companionship, or perhaps provide special music. It is important not to bring too many outside people, though, so that residents don't feel overwhelmed.

Keep in mind before you start that interruptions are likely to occur. Be flexible. These are folks who may have lost their inhibitions and abilities to know what is appropriate and what is not. Having some volunteers who can sit amongst people, offering support and comfort, will help. If someone needs a drink, seems distressed, or needs a restroom break, the volunteer can locate a caregiver to assist. Don't let possible interruptions deter you. The more often you go to the facility to hold such services, the more familiar and comfortable you'll all be with one another. Roll with the punches and don't feel stressed if things don't go as planned or need some last-minute modifying. Everyone will be blessed.

The following service is designed especially for people in the middle to late stages of dementia. (You could perform a similar service for people in the early stages; simply add more substance to your sermon and perhaps a few more hymns.) The more interactive it can be, the better. Always put components in the service that residents can say and do: familiar Scripture, prayer, songs, poems, or other elements.

Twenty to thirty minutes is the optimal length.

SUGGESTED ORDER OF SERVICE

Play hymns as people arrive.

If a musician cannot be present, use a CD player or another electronic device. Music immediately triggers the familiarity of hearing hymns play before worship at church and it will set a reverent tone, readying people for worship. Simple musical arrangements are the best, so participants can clearly hear the melody. They can listen or sing along as they wait for everyone to gather. If possible, arrange people in a semicircle around the worship leader. A semicircle creates an informal setting where everyone can see each other.

Once everyone has arrived, the worship leader should greet each person individually.

The worship leader begins by shaking hands or touching each person on the arm, introducing himself and thanking participants for coming to worship. By doing this, the leader not only sets a friendly tone but also focuses each person's attention as he proceeds from one person to the next. This is important because people living with dementia are easily distractible. By the time the leader greets everyone, they'll be more focused, at least momentarily, on the start of worship.

When planning the worship service, it is important to make choices based on the familiarity of the attendees. Depending upon age, many people experiencing dementia may be most familiar with a particular biblical interpretation. In the example below, I chose the King James Version for this reason. Your traditions may vary.

Leader: "Good morning. Let's begin our worship time by saying the Lord's Prayer together."

Say the prayer slowly and distinctly with worshipers. When it is completed, comment on how nice it was to hear everyone saying this prayer together, how even though we come from different places and different churches, this was the prayer we probably learned as children. It is the prayer Jesus taught his disciples when he was teaching them to pray.

Leader: "It's also good to begin our worship time by saying a scripture together. Let's say Psalm 118:24: 'This is the day which the LORD hath made; we will rejoice and be glad in it'" (KJV). (Repeat, encouraging participants to join in with you.)

Remind worshipers that each day is a gift from God. You might talk briefly about whatever particular day it is, putting the day into context of weather, season, holiday, or special occasion. Talk about how every day is a day to thank God for his presence and care. Each day is an occasion to be kind and loving toward others because God loves us and shows us how to love.

You might, of course, select a different scripture to recite and briefly explain. I have found, though, that this simple, joyful verse is familiar to most people. It sets a positive, thankful tone as we enter worship. I use it at the beginning of every worship time, and now our residents in memory care have come to expect it. They respond well to structure and predictability. When I began leading worship using this verse years ago, some people were not familiar and couldn't recite the words. Amazingly, those same folks, who are living with dementia, have learned it through repetition and now recite with me loudly each week.

Leader: "Now we're going to sing one of the first hymns we probably all learned as children. This hymn talks of Jesus's love for us. Can anyone guess what it is?"

(The residents will guess, and most will be able to sing it.) Ideally, you would want to have a volunteer pianist who could come from your church and play. If not, singing along with a recording or a cappella is fine.

Sing "Jesus Loves Me."

Sermon

Provide a five- to ten-minute devotional thought that appeals to the senses and is interactive. The example below uses the theme of "God's Creation." At the end of this sample worship service you will find other suggestions for the devotional theme.

GOD'S CREATION

Take seashells around for folks to feel. (Other weeks, you might give each person a laminated calendar page containing a different seasonal scene, bird feathers, sand, leaves in fall, flowers in spring. Be creative.) Let people see, touch, and smell the items, as appropriate. Go to them one at a time and have a very brief conversation about the item they're holding. Hold it up for all to see, or go around as you're talking and let everyone see and touch it. (Most people will watch as you go from one person to the next.)

In this way you involve group members in participating. Participation is essential for engagement. It's okay if someone falls asleep while holding their item and drops it or wants to cling to it when you come to them. Just pick it up or let them continue to hold on to it. When you want to get it later, they may relinquish it easily, or you could offer something else in exchange. (Beware of giving small items if you know a person has a tendency to put things in his mouth.)

Read Scripture from Genesis 1 when talking about creation, or a psalm that talks about creation. Talk with the attendees about how they see God in nature. What do they like most about nature? Was anyone a gardener? Some people will be able to respond with brief answers. Go up to people in the semicircle one-on-one. If they can't answer, make suggestions to which they can nod or shake their heads, such as:

"I love feeling the sand between my toes. Do you?"

"I love seeing new baby animals in spring. Do you?"

"I enjoy feeling warm sunshine on my face. How about you?"

"I like to hear rain falling on a tin roof. Is that something you enjoy, too?"

This kind of questioning allows people to participate who can no long speak much or carry on conversation.

Sing hymns that go with the theme of the worship time/devotional.

Select a couple hymns such as:

- "How Great Thou Art"

- "For the Beauty of the Earth"

- "All Things Bright and Beautiful"

- "All Creatures of Our God and King"

Ask participants about things in nature they are thankful for, and repeat what they say so all can hear.

Introduce a prayer time and ask if there are any prayer requests.

Some people will speak requests, while others won't be capable. After you've received requests, suggest some unmentioned things they all might like to pray for such as family, friends, food, a nice place to live, pets, warm blankets. You'll see people nodding affirmation. These are words they might say, if they are able.

Pray, and mention the prayer requests that were spoken.

Close with a final hymn.

Over time you'll discover the group's "favorite." As we end each service, we always sing "In the Garden." I've found that most people sing it with joy.

Include quiet music playing as you go around to each individual, thanking them for coming and offering an individual blessing.

For example, you might say: "I'm so glad you were here today, Mrs. Brown. Thank you for coming. God loves you so much and will always be with you. Have a blessed day."

ADDITIONAL THEMES, SCRIPTURE, AND HYMN IDEAS USING A SIMILAR ORDER OF WORSHIP FROM THE EXAMPLE ABOVE

God's Love for All People

Scripture: John 3:16

Read, and then invite them to recite it with you.

Visuals: Show pictures of people and places from around the world. Give each resident a picture to hold. Intersperse showing each person's picture and briefly talking about the picture with singing verses of "He's Got the Whole World in His Hands."

Hymns:
- "This is My Father's World"
- "Jesus Loves the Little Children, All the Children of the World"
- "God's Beautiful World"

Music for listening or singing:
- "What a Wonderful World"

Praising God

Scripture: Psalm 100

Read and then invite them to recite it with you, if they are able.

Visuals: Pass out various easy-to-play musical instruments such as tambourines, maracas, flutes, or kazoos. Include items to wave such as banners, flags or scarves. Incorporate playing the instruments and waving the items in rhythm with the music.

Hymns:
- "Holy, Holy, Holy"
- "Praise God from Whom All Blessings Flow"

- "Now Thank We All Our God"
- "Praise to the Lord the Almighty"
- "Amazing Grace"

God's Presence

Scripture: Psalm 139

Read the scripture passage to the group and talk about how God's presence is with us always.

Visuals: Bring a stuffed bunny and Margaret Wise Brown's book, *The Runaway Bunny*. Read the book and talk about God's presence with us like the mother rabbit with her small bunny.

Hymns:
- "What a Friend We Have in Jesus"
- "Great Is Thy Faithfulness"
- "Abide with Me"

Other possible themes:

- Heaven
- Forgiveness
- Love
- Friendship
- Family
- Peace
- Joy
- Grace

CONCLUSION

$\mathcal{M}$inistering as a chaplain to people with dementia and their families began for me during clinical pastoral education training at a large metropolitan hospital. As part of a geriatric psychiatry team, I visited patients on the hospital's geriatric psychiatry floor and in skilled nursing care and assisted living facilities. Until then, I hadn't been around people with dementia much, and had heard it predominantly referred to as "hardening of the arteries" or "senility." Aside from doing regular rounds, I was referred to visit patients who talked about church, religion, or spiritual needs to other team members.

One of my first days there, I was asked to go see Mrs. Foster as soon as possible. When I arrived in her room, Mrs. Foster was hallucinating and sobbing. In the confusion of her mind, she was distraught about something going on at her church. In jumbled words, she was talking about "the minister . . . his wife . . . danger . . . at church . . . a burglar . . . a gun." I stood at the door to her room, watching her and literally quaking in my boots. I prayed that God would show me what to do, because I sure didn't know.

It was a pivotal moment for me.

After listening to and observing her for a few minutes, I quietly slid into the room and sat on the edge of the bed. She was rocking and sobbing in the chair next me. For a few more moments I continued listening to her talk. I can honestly admit being scared to death. I just knew I would do the wrong thing and make things worse.

After a few moments I reached over and gently touched her arm.

"Hello, Mrs. Foster," I began. "I'm Kathy, the chaplain. It sounds like something terrible is happening. Would you like for me to pray with you about it?"

She sniffed and quietly said, "Yes."

If I knew then what I know now, I would not have reached out and touched her on the arm. In Mrs. Foster's frenzied state, she could have easily hit me when I did that. I was a stranger coming into her space, her literal time of terror. But she didn't lash out at me physically. She accepted my offer to pray with her. Since she was so concerned about something that was happening to her minister at her church, I prayed with her about that. If I were that worried and upset, I reasoned, I would pray. I thought that might help her, too.

I prayed specifically about the reality of the situation she was so concerned about, not knowing that this was what she needed. Those words just came out of my mouth. I prayed that God would protect her minister and his wife. I prayed that God would help Mrs. Foster feel His loving presence, too. Gradually, as I prayed with her, her breathing became more regular and her hysterical sobs became muted cries. Sitting with her for a few more minutes,

I eventually released the hand she'd let me hold and told her I needed to go but would be back later.

The next day in our team meeting, I learned from the social worker that she had spoken with the patient's family, describing the patient's distress. The family recalled what had happened in the 1940s at her church: A burglar broke into the church, and shot and killed her minister and his wife. For some reason, Mrs. Foster had been reliving that experience.

I truly believe the Holy Spirit interceded on my behalf, guiding me. At that time, I was a rookie chaplain with a lot of learning to do.

I learned valuable lessons that day that have informed my ministry for all these years.

Enter into the reality of the person you're visiting who has dementia. She cannot come to yours.

Help them access their faith when they are having trouble initiating faith practices that would provide comfort, peace, joy, and connection to God.

Do not be afraid to visit someone, even if it might mean saying or doing the wrong thing before you find the right thing. God is with us always.

As you seek to serve, in Christ's name, may you be empowered with God's grace and peace. May you feel God's presence in tangible ways as you trust God's guidance and boldly go. God says, "Be not afraid! I go before you always! Come, follow me."

Many blessings,
Kathy

To purchase the accompanying *When Words Fail* instructional DVD and download the free study guide, please visit our website at www. whenwordsfail.com.

NOTES

Introduction

1   Alzheimer's Association, "2016 Alzheimer's Disease Facts and Figures," *Alzheimer's and Dementia* 12, no. 4 (2016).

Chapter 1

1   Pew Research Center, "Religious Landscape Study," https//www.pewforum. org/religious-landscape-study.

2   Alzheimer's Association, "2016 Alzheimer's Disease Facts and Figures."

Chapter 2

*   The image of the brain in Chapter 2 is taken from Blausen.com staff, "Blausen gallery 2014," *Wikiversity Journal of Medicine,* https://en.wikiversity.org/wiki/ WikiJournal_of_Medicine/Medical_gallery_of_Blausen_Medical_2014 [CC BY 3.0 (http://creativecommons.org/licenses/by/3.0)], via Wikimedia Commons.

1   Alzheimer's Association, "2016 Alzheimer's Disease Facts and Figures."

2   Ibid.

3   Ibid.

4   Ibid.

Chapter 3

1   Ibid.

Chapter 8

1   Ibid.

2   Ibid.

3   Ibid.

4   Ibid.

5   Ibid.

6   See Helpguide.org, "Senior Housing: Your Guide to Assisted Living Facilities, Independent Living, and Other Housing Options," http://www.helpguide. org/articles/senior-housing/assisted-living-facilities.htm; and Westminster Canterbury Richmond, "Having the Conversation," http://www.wcrichmond. org/having-the-conversation.

Chapter 9

1   Pew Research Center, "Baby Boomers Retire," December 29, 2010, http:// www.pewresearch.org/daily-number/baby-boomers-retire.

2   Alzheimer's Association, "2016 Alzheimer's Disease Facts and Figures."

3   The Alzheimer's Disease Education and Referral Center, 1-800-438-4380; Rarediseases.info.nih.gov; Alzheimer's Prevention Registry, endalznow.org; and the Brain Health Registry, brainhealthregistry.org.

4   First United Methodist Church, Montgomery, AL, "Respite Ministry," www. fumcmontgomery.org/respite (accessed Jan. 17, 2018).

5   Dr. Mark Patterson and Joanne Sherman, interview with the author, January 14, 2018, Midlothian, VA.

6   Giving Voice Chorus, "About Giving Voice," www.givingvoicechorus.org/ about (accessed Jan. 17, 2018).

7   MacPhail Center for Music, "Impact of Music: Creative Aging," www. macphail.org/impact-of-music/creative-aging (accessed Jan. 17, 2018).

8   "Chorus for People with Dementia and Their Caregivers," *YouTube*, uploaded by Musicoterapia Online, https://www.youtube.com/watch?v=7vSRk9Sbk1Q (accessed Jan. 17, 2018).

9   Richard Byrne. "Healing Measures," *Peabody Magazine*, Johns Hopkins University (Spring 2017), 15–19.

10   "Chorus for People with Dementia and Their Caregivers."

RESOURCES FOR SPIRITUAL CARE AND DEMENTIA

Alzheimer's Association. "2016 Alzheimer's Disease Facts and Figures," *Alzheimer's & Dementia* 11, no. 3 (2015), 332+. (Available at www.alz.org/facts.)

Atchley, Robert. *Spirituality and Aging.* Baltimore: The Johns Hopkins University Press, 2009.

Binstock, Robert, Stephen Post, and Peter Whitehouse, eds. *Dementia and Aging: Ethics, Values, and Policy Choices.* Baltimore: Johns Hopkins University Press, 1992.

Brackey, Jolene. *Creating Moments of Joy for the Person with Alzheimer's or Dementia.* 4th ed. West Lafayette, IN: Purdue University Press, 2007. (Available at www.enhancedmoments.com.)

Brown, Margaret Wise. *The Runaway Bunny.* New York: Harper & Row Publishers, Inc., 1942.

Broyles, Frank. *Coach Broyles' Playbook for Alzheimer's Caregivers: A Practical Tips Guide,* 2006, www.alzheimersplaybook.com.

Burdick, Lydia. *The Sunshine on My Face: A Read-Aloud Book for Memory-Challenged Adults.* Baltimore: Health Professions Press, 2004.

ClergyAgainstAlzheimer's Network. *Seasons of Caring: Meditations for Alzheimer's and Dementia Caregivers*. Chevy Chase, MD: ClergyAgainstAlzheimer's Network, 2014.

Coste, Joanne Koenig. *Learning to Speak Alzheimer's: A Groundbreaking Approach for Everyone Dealing with the Disease*. Boston: Houghton Mifflin Company, 2004.

Dill, Robin. *Walking with Grace: Tools for Implementing and Launching a Congregational Respite Program*. Bloomington, NY: iUniverse, Inc., 2009.

Feil, Naomi. *The Validation Breakthrough: Simple Techniques for Communicating with People with Alzheimer's-Type Dementia*. Baltimore: Health Professions Press, 1993.

Gwyther, Lisa P. *You Are One of Us: Successful Clergy/Church Connections to Alzheimer's Families*. Durham, NC: Duke University Medical Center, 1995.

Hornback, Paul M. *God Still Remembers Me: Devotions for Facing Alzheimer's Disease with Faith*. Rochester: New York: Starry Night Publishing.com. 2015.

Hunt, Angela Elwell. *The Tale of Three Trees: A Traditional Folktale*. Colorado Springs: Lion Publishing, 1989.

Kimble, Melvin A., Susan McFadden, et al., eds. *Aging, Spirituality, and Religion: A Handbook*. Volumes I and II. Minneapolis: Fortress Press. 2002.

MacKinlay, Elizabeth, ed. *Ageing and Spirituality across Faiths and Cultures*. London: Jessica Kingsley Publishers, 2010.

Mast, Benjamin. *Second Forgetting*. Grand Rapids: Zondervan, 2014.

McCarthy, Bernie. *Hearing the Person with Dementia: Person-Centered Approaches to Communication for Families and Caregivers*. London: Jessica Kingsley Publishers, 2011.

McKim, Donald K., ed. *God Never Forgets: Faith, Hope, and Alzheimer's Disease*. Louisville: Westminster Knox Press. 1997.

Murphey, Cecil. *When Someone You Love Has Alzheimer's: Daily Encouragement*. Kansas City, Missouri: Beacon Hill Press. 2004.

Muth, Jon. *The Three Questions: Based on a Story by Leo Tolstoy*. New York: Scholastic Press, 2002.

National Institute on Aging. *Alzheimer's Disease: Unraveling the Mystery,* https://www.free-ebooks.net/ebook/Alzheimer-s-Disease-Unraveling-the-Mystery (updated annually).

National Institute on Aging. *Understanding Memory Loss: What to Do When You Have Trouble Remembering* (May 2013). https://order.nia.nih.gov/sites/default/files/2017-07/Understanding-MemoryLoss_508.pdf.

National Institutes of Health. *The Dementias: Hope through Research*. NIH Publication No. 13-2252 (September 2013).

Ray, Cynthia. "Remember Those Who Forget: Becoming a Dementia-Friendly Congregation." *The Presbyterian Outlook* 198, no. 1 (January 4, 2016): 10–13.

Sapp, Stephen. *When Alzheimer's Disease Strikes*. Palm Beach, FL: Desert Ministries, Inc., 2002.

Schaefer, Robert B. *Alzheimer's: The Identity Thief of the 21st Century*. Baltimore: PublishAmerica, 2010.

Shamy, Eileen. *A Guide to the Spiritual Dimension of Care for People with Alzheimer's Disease and Related Dementias*. Philadelphia: Jessica Kingsley Publishers, 2003.

Swinton, John. *Dementia: Living in the Memories of God*. Grand Rapids: William B. Eerdmans Publishing Company, 2012.

Thibault, Jane Marie and Morgan, Richard. *No Act of Love Is Ever Wasted: The Spirituality of Caring for Persons with Dementia*. Nashville: Upper Room Books. 2009.

VandeCreek, Larry. *Spiritual Care of Persons with Dementia: Fundamentals of Pastoral Practice*. New York: W. H. Freeman & Company, 1999.

Conversations about End of Life and Advance Directives:

- www.agingwithdignity.org

- www.4070talk.com

- www.theconversationproject.org

Websites:

- www.alz.org

- www.archrespite.org

- www.caregiverslibrary.org

- www.caregiverstress.com

- www.caring.com

- www.eldercare.gov

- www.episcopalchurch.org/files/Aging

- www.episcopalchurch.org/page/older-adult-ministries

- www.HomeInstead.com

- www.leadingage.org

- www.nia.nih.gov/alzheimers

- www.poamn.org/index.php/older-adult-ministries-planning-guide/

- www.rosalynncarter.org

- www.thiscaringhome.org

- www.wcrichmond.org

- *When Words Fail*: www.whenwordsfail.com. Please use this site to share your experiences.

ABOUT THE AUTHOR

Rev. Kathy Fogg Berry received a Masters of Religious Education from Southern Seminary in Louisville, Kentucky, and a Masters in Patient Counseling and a postgraduate certificate in aging studies from Virginia Commonwealth University in Richmond, Virginia. She has served as a chaplain in a variety of long-term care and hospice settings and as a trainer for the Alzheimer's Association. She serves at Westminster Canterbury Richmond, where she provides spiritual care and creates memory-support projects with residents, their families, and the staff who care for them. She teaches the *When Words Fail* seminar for clergy and lay leaders, and speaks regionally and nationally about spirituality and dementia.